The Atheist's Primer

Michael Palmer

The Lutterworth Press

The Lutterworth Press
P.O. Box 60
Cambridge
CB1 2NT
United Kingdom

www.lutterworth.com
publishing@lutterworth.com

ISBN: 978 0 7188 9297 5

British Library Cataloguing in Publication Data
A record is available from the British Library

Copyright © Michael Palmer, 2012

First Published, 2012

The Atheist's Creed

I BELIEVE THAT the cosmos is all that is or ever was or ever will be.

I BELIEVE THAT no other reality, divine or otherwise, exists. There is no life after death, no meaning to life apart from life, and no events or experiences, individuals or scriptures by which any supra-natural reality can be revealed. The cosmos forms the boundary of our experience.

I BELIEVE THAT human life has no meaning apart from itself: that while there is purpose in life, there is no purpose to life. There is no ultimate justice, no final act of grace and no salvation. This is not a providential universe.

I BELIEVE THAT not everything is permissible. For while that which increases happiness is not always a good, that which increases misery is always an evil.

I BELIEVE THAT by the deployment of reason and the acquisition of knowledge, by the development of moral law and the cultivation of compassion, the suffering of humanity can be alleviated and the condition of our lives improved.

I BELIEVE THAT the path to individual and collective happiness lies in being educated to reality, and in being thus released from the irresponsible and pernicious illusion of religion, for which there is neither evidence nor need.

For five friends from Durham University:
David Allott, Martyn Trahair, Raymonde Robinson,
and Roger and Fiona Bonfield

Contents

Introduction

Atheism is currently enjoying the limelight, both in academic circles and in the popular press. The so-called 'new atheists' are in vogue, and books like Richard Dawkins' *The God Delusion* (2006), Daniel Dennett's *Breaking the Spell* (2006), Sam Harris' *The End of Faith* (2004) and his *Letter to a Christian Nation* (2006) and the two volumes published in 2007 by the late Christopher Hitchens – *God is not Great* and his wide-ranging anthology *The Portable Atheist* – have caught the public imagination. Unsurprisingly, believers have not been slow to enter the lists. Alister McGrath has countered with his *The Twilight of Atheism* (2004) and with two books on Dawkins – *Dawkin's God* (2004) and *The Dawkins Delusion* (2007); and mention should also be made of Keith Ward's *Is Religion Dangerous?* (2006) and Francis Collins' *The Language of God* (2006), the last-named being subtitled 'A Scientist Presents Evidence for Belief,' which gives a clear indication of its general thrust. Nor does it take much time on the internet to see how international this debate has become and how acrimonious.

At the centre of this controversy stands the well-worn debate between science and religion, a debate that highlights the differing methods by which each discipline seeks to obtain knowledge. The charge levelled against religion is that faith never places itself within the cold light of empirical confirmation, and so is free to wander off unhindered into its own private world of fantastical delusions; and the charge against the scientist is that the limitation of knowledge to only that which may be observed and verified is a restriction that cannot be sustained: that scientific truth can lay no claims to infallibility and that it straightjackets the scope of our experiences, which may include, after all, not just religious experiences but also moral, aesthetic and psychological experiences as well, none of which can be easily confirmed or refuted solely by reference to observed facts and the evidence of the senses.

This old controversy between science and orthodoxy has been considerably sharpened, however, by the emergence of Charles Darwin (1809-1882) as the central protagonist. For Dawkins and his allies, Darwin's achievement is on a par with those of Galileo, Newton and Einstein, and the evolutionary process that he unravelled is as near to a scientific fact as we are ever likely to discover. But the theory of natural selection that Darwin presents is one of unparalleled barbarity, impersonal and haphazard in form and subject only to the vagaries of environment; and this picture, so the neo-Darwinians contend, is totally at variance with any notion of an omnipotent, benevolent and purposive deity, of a loving God who cares for his creatures but who is yet quite prepared to subject them to a life of unremitting brutality and hardship. To put the matter more strongly: if Darwin is right, then it would appear that we have here an irreducible *incompatibility* between scientific evidence and religious belief which no amount of theological ingenuity can resolve. Chance cannot accommodate design and cruelty cannot accommodate benevolence, at least not on this scale, on the scale of omnipotence, when presumably other options were available to God and the creation of a happier and less barbaric world a real possibility. The only rational conclusion to draw from this, so the argument runs, is that the theistic case should be jettisoned altogether.

These are important matters and I shall refer to them again. There is, however, one further feature of the current debate to notice. With Darwin centre stage, and given the scientific backgrounds of most parties to the dispute, it is entirely understandable that arguments of a more overtly *philosophical* stamp should remain in the background; and this despite the fact that it is these which, by and large, have provided the principal landmarks in the history of atheism. This has produced some puzzling, and at times exasperating, results, and they are to be seen on both sides of the dispute. If we look again at McGrath's *The Twilight of Atheism*, with its subheading 'The Rise and Fall of Disbelief in the Modern World', we notice with some astonishment that this argument is sustained without any consideration whatsoever of the work of David Hume (1711-1776) – a quite extraordinary omission, given that Hume is, by common consent, the architect of the most damaging philosophical critique of theistic rationality ever devised. But whereas Hume is mentioned just twice in passing, fourteen pages are devoted to Madalyn Murray O'Hair (1919-1995), the founder of *American Atheists*, and to her exposure as a 'crude and abusive spirit.'[1] I think that McGrath establishes his point: O'Hair was probably unpleasant – a conclusion from which we may infer that 'Some atheists are unpleasant'. But quite where this gets us is hard to see. For atheists, after all, have no monopoly of unpleasantness.

But similar omissions are evident on the other side. What McGrath includes, some atheists exclude. The most startling omission here is of Friedrich Nietzsche (1844-1900), who hardly gets a mention from any of the authors I have so far cited. This is very strange, and its strangeness

1   *Ibid.*, New York & London, Galilee & Doubleday, 2006, p.255.

lies in the fact that what has here been excluded remains perhaps the most potent force within the whole arsenal of continental atheism and indeed provides an entirely different brand of atheism from that found within, say, the tradition of British empiricism. Nietzsche is unconcerned about discussions to do with whether belief has or has not any evidential support – and to that extent he would regard the work of Dawkins as an intellectual cul-de-sac – and is much more concerned with questions to do with the 'death of God', with the moral and psychological implications for human beings once this tremendous fact – that there is no God – has been accepted. Nietzsche's influence, which I shall discuss later at some length, also provides an important corrective to the impression, so easily gained, that the 'new atheism' is exclusively an Anglo-Saxon phenomenon. But such is not the case, as is evidenced by the French philosopher Michel Onfray's hair-raising polemic *In Defence of Atheism* (2007), which is set quite deliberately within a Nietzschean mould.

My intention, then, is to bring some of these important philosophical arguments to the fore, and to provide a selective overview of the extraordinary richness of the atheistic literature, which extends from the time of the ancient Greeks down to our own day. Among the many authors cited there are many familiar and unfamiliar names, with four authors singled out for more extended treatment: David Hume, Nietzsche, Karl Marx and Sigmund Freud. It goes without saying that for each of their arguments there is a theistic response, but to include them as well would have made this a very big book indeed – although I should add in defence that many of these counter-arguments are presented in the two volumes of my *The Philosophy of Religion* (Lutterworth, 2008, and published by Viking Press of Minneapolis in one volume, 2010). I am also grateful to the publishers, Routledge, for giving me permission to make extensive use of two other publications of mine – *Freud and Jung on Religion* (1997) and *The Question of God* (2001).

The Atheist's Primer is an abridgement of my *The Atheist's Creed* (2010), omitting entirely the primary source material – original texts drawn from the time of the Ancient Greeks to the present-day – and the extensive range of biographical and bibliographical information accompanying those texts. While I hope this material provided a useful scholarly guide to the literature, it was felt to be rather surplus to requirements for a more general readership. At any rate, all that has now been jettisoned; and I have retained only my Introductions, for the most part unchanged, and a slightly modified Guide to Further Reading that now stands that the end of the book. The result is well under half the original length, requiring, as before, no specialist knowledge of philosophy, with any unavoidable philosophical jargon kept down to an absolute minimum.

I am grateful to my friend, Paul Keyte, Headmaster, for pointing out some infelicities in the original edition and these have now been corrected. I am also grateful to the editor of this volume, Oliver Barham, and to Adrian Brink, the Managing Director of The Lutterworth Press, for their encouragement and advice. It is worth recording that my connection with The Lutterworth Press at Cambridge now reaches back to 1991, with the publication of my *Moral Problems*, and I am pleased to record that it has been an entirely amicable association from that day to this. The fact that The Lutterworth Press is one of the oldest Christian publishing houses in the world, which started life in 1799 as The Religious Tract Society, makes its publication of *The Atheist's Creed* and *The Atheist's Primer* a further indication, if ever one was needed, of the remarkable breadth of its interests.

The Atheist's Creed began with my own opening statement, fashioned like a creed; and this I have retained for *The Atheist's Primer*. I am well aware that this may create difficulties. Atheism itself is not all of a piece, and some atheists will claim that theirs is not a belief-system at all but a matter of demonstrable fact. I realize also that in composition my creed will appear to some far too bland, lacking any kind of rhetorical resonance, such as we find in the familiar creeds of the liturgy. But this is quite intentional. To each proposition of my creed could be added innumerable sub-clauses: about the nature of the universe, the complexities of our evolving world, the autonomy of individuals, and so on; but all these I have avoided, partly through fear of succumbing to platitudinous overload, and partly because I wanted to keep to the strictest and least controversial minimum, providing only the barest outline of atheism's landscape and of what I take to be its core beliefs.

Michael Palmer

1
The Meaning of Atheism

i. Atheism: A Definition

The word 'atheism' is a translation of the Greek *atheos*, which combines the prefix *a* (meaning 'not' or 'without') with *theos* (meaning 'god'). Accordingly the term is most commonly employed as 'disbelief in, or denial of, the existence of God'. However, this definition is not as straightforward as it appears. In the first place, and most obviously, what is being disbelieved in or denied will change according to the various definitions of God being employed. Thus atheism from the standpoint of the Christian religion, which believes in a personal God who is the one supreme personal being and creator of the universe, will be a very different conception in contrast to atheism as understood by a deist, a polytheist or pantheist. In the second place, and historically, we find that the term 'atheistic' has frequently been applied to denote nothing more than trivial dogmatic differences. 'Atheist' now stands as a term of abuse directed by one party to a theological dispute against another. So we read in Psalm 14:1 that 'the fool hath said in his heart, there is no God' – a declaration immortalised by Anselm of Canterbury in his ontological argument for God's existence;[1] but this is no philosophical justification for God's existence but is referring, more simply, to those with a practical disbelief in God's government of human affairs, manifested in disobedience to moral laws – as the Psalmist continues, such people are 'corrupt' and have 'done abominable works'. Other more notable examples suggest themselves. Baruch de Spinoza (1632-1677), condemned as the 'greatest atheist', was expelled from the Jewish community in Amsterdam not because he denied God's existence but because he committed the 'abominable heresy' of denying the providential God of scripture and of identifying the deity with the causal mechanisms of the universe. More problematic is the case of Spinoza's English contemporary, Thomas Hobbes (1588-1679). In 1666 a committee of the House of Commons was convened to investigate his alleged atheism. Hobbes was terrified and burnt many

1 See below, p.33

Thomas Hobbes

of his unpublished manuscripts; but again the reason given for the enquiry was not because he denied God – for Hobbes God is the 'first cause' of the universe, although admittedly by means totally incomprehensible to us – but because he asserts that God, as 'the most real substance that exists', must be a material entity and so have a body, an heretical conclusion contrary to the Thirty-Nine Articles of the Anglican Church. These misuses of the term 'atheist' are, admittedly, of almost no philosophical consequence and retain an historical interest only; but in the light of them one can certainly understand why some, in order to avoid these pejorative associations, have, like J.C.A. Gaskin, abandoned the term 'atheism' altogether in favour of the more neutral 'unbelief.'[2]

There is, however, another much more important ambiguity to reveal. If our opening definition construes 'atheism' as '*without* theism', then perhaps we should more properly regard an atheist *not* as someone who believes there is no God but as someone who is more simply *without theism*. In other words, perhaps we should agree that an atheist is *not* someone who, having tested the appropriate theological arguments, concludes that these arguments are spurious and that no such being exists; but rather, that an atheist is someone marked by the *absence of belief*: he or she simply *has no belief in God*. On these terms, the atheist is, properly speaking, not concerned with the matter of God at all. For how can one repudiate something when one has no conception of what one is denying?

According to *The Encyclopedia of Unbelief*, it is this position, now commonly known as *negative atheism*, which the great majority of atheists adopt. Most atheists, we are told, would agree with Charles Bradlaugh (1833-1891), the most prominent of nineteenth-century English atheists, when he writes:

> Atheism is without God. It does not assert no God. The atheist does not say that there is no God, but he says 'I know not what you mean by God. I am without the idea of God. The word God to me is a sound conveying no clear or distinct affirmation. I do

---

2   *Varieties of Unbelief*, ed. J.C.A. Gaskin, London, Collier Macmillan, 1989, pp. 1-2.

not deny God, because I cannot deny that of which I have no conception, and the conception of which by its affirmer is so imperfect that he is unable to define it for me.[3]

Many distinguished atheists of the past have subscribed to negative atheism: for example, Richard Carlisle (1790-1843), Charles Southwell (1814-1860) and Annie Besant (1847-1933). The earliest of these, Baron d'Holbach (1723-1789) – someone we shall meet later on as the author of the first avowedly atheistic publication, *The System of Nature* (1770)[4] – goes so far as to claim that, if atheism is having no belief in God, then we should regard all uninformed children as atheists – a claim rejected by

Antony Flew

Ernest Nagel. Nagel claims that atheism must involve some denial of theistic propositions and so cannot apply either to children or indeed to adults indifferent to the whole question of God's existence.[5]

Two modern exponents of negative atheism should be mentioned. The first is George H. Smith in *Atheism: The Case Against God* (1979). Smith offers a further and widely used description of negative atheism as 'implicit atheism': 'An implicit atheist', he writes, 'is a person who does not believe in a god, but who has not explicitly rejected or denied the truth of theism. Implicit atheism does not require familiarity with the idea of a god'.[6] So Smith agrees with d'Holbach (and not with Nagel) that, on these terms, children qualify as atheists. The second exponent of negative atheism is Antony Flew in his influential article 'The Presumption of Atheism' (1976). According to Flew, negative atheism, precisely because it is without belief, places the burden of proof

---

3   *The Freethinkers Text Book*, London, 1876. Quoted in *The Encyclopedia of Unbelief*, Buffalo, New York, Prometheus Books, 1985, p.28.
4   See below, pp.42-44
5   'Philosophical Concepts of Atheism', in J.E. Fairchild (ed.), *Basic Beliefs: The Religious Philosophies of Mankind*, Dobbs Ferry, NY, Sheridan House, 1959, 1987, pp.173-192. See also *The Atheist's Creed*, Cambridge, The Lutterworth Press, 2010, pp.20-25. Hereafter cited as *TAC*.
6   Buffalo, New York, Prometheus Books, 1989, pp.13-14.

squarely upon those with belief. This is a methodological presumption, and follows from the fact that, just as with the legal presumption of innocence, the onus is on those to demonstrative the positive – that X has done Y – and not on those to demonstrate the negative. We should proceed, therefore, as if we are in a court of law and hold to the old legal axiom that 'The onus of proof lies on the man who affirms, not on the man who denies'. What is thereafter required is sufficient evidence to establish that the presumption of innocence is misplaced and that one can establish such-and-such to be the case, not because one believes this to be true but because one knows this to be true.[7]

> It is by reference to this inescapable demand for grounds that the presumption of atheism is justified. If it is to be established that there is a God, then we have to have good grounds for believing that this is indeed so. Until and unless some such grounds are produced we have literally no reason at all for believing; and in that situation the only reasonable posture must be that of either the negative atheist or the agnostic. So the onus of proof has to rest on the proposition. It must be up to them: first, to give whatever sense they choose to the word 'God', meeting any objection that so defined it would relate only to an incoherent pseudo-concept; and, second, to bring forward sufficient reasons to warrant their claim that, in their present sense of the word 'God', there is a God. The same applies, with appropriate alterations, if what is to be made out is, not that theism is known to be true, but only – more modestly – that it can be seen to be at least more or less probable.[8]

However, not all atheists agree with *The Encyclopedia of Unbelief* and are unwilling to concede to negative atheism the majority view. For there is another version of atheism which, far from denoting an absence of God, specifies a detailed and intended repudiation of all theistic claims, replacing one belief-system with a system of its own. This is positive atheism, sometimes also known as speculative atheism, the central claim of which is that there is no God. George Smith calls this 'explicit atheism': the explicit atheist, he says, 'is one who rejects belief in a god. This deliberate and rational rejection presupposes familiarity with theistic beliefs and is sometimes characterized as anti-theism'.[9] Positive or explicit atheism, in other words, by consciously denying God's existence, knows full well what is about, and provides within the history of ideas those full-scale frontal

---

7   *The Presumption of Atheism and Other Essays*, London, Elek/Pemberton, 1976, p. 18. See also *TAC*: 26-33.

8   *Ibid.*, p.30.

9   *Op.cit.*, p.17.

assaults upon the claims of religion by which atheism is more generally characterized. On this reading the heavyweights of the atheistic tradition – Feuerbach, Marx, Schopenhauer, Nietzsche, Freud and Sartre, and in our own day, Ernest Nagel, Richard Dawkins, Michael Martin and Daniel Dennett – are all positive atheists in the sense that each provides, in their own distinctive way, grounds for the repudiation of God. Viewed in this light, the suggestion that all children are atheists becomes inappropriate. For uninstructed children, not

Thomas Huxley

knowing God, can say nothing about God one way or the other, and are therefore in no position to reject (or indeed support) any theistic claims. But this cannot be said of positive atheists or indeed of believers themselves. For when a Christian rejects, say, the gods of Hinduism, he or she presumably has reasons for this rejection, and so acts, towards the Hindu at least, as a positive atheist. In this respect, all theists act like positive atheists when they provide grounds for denying the existence of all other gods except their own.

ii. Atheism and Agnosticism

One final terminological confusion remains to be cleared up. This is between atheism and *agnosticism*. The term combines the familiar Greek prefix '*a*' ('not' or 'without') with '*gnosis*' (knowledge), and affirms the fairly common view that the agnostic is someone who, in the absence of knowledge, neither believes nor disbelieves in the existence of God, and that he or she is therefore 'without belief'. This being so, the agnostic, while clearly not subscribing to the anti-theistic beliefs of positive atheism, is sometimes presented as a type of negative atheist, as someone for whom the question of God simply does not arise. And certainly, understood in this way, agnosticism is compatible with negative atheism. For clearly there is no incompatibility between saying 'I have no belief' and 'I neither believe nor disbelieve in God.' But this compatibility is misleading. Strictly speaking, the term 'agnostic', as originally coined in 1869 by Thomas Huxley (1825-1895) enshrines, to quote Huxley himself, 'not a creed but a method, the essence of which lies in the rigorous application of a single principle'. This principle is 'to follow reason as far as it can take you', and is much more restrictive that it might appear; for, as Huxley understands it, the principle imposes a *limitation* on the scope of human knowledge – this limitation being that we can have knowledge of 'real phenomena' only, and that so far as what may lie behind or beyond such phenomena is concerned – whether it be God or any transcendent level of reality – we should suspend judgment because there is no evidence which entitles us to deny or affirm anything. Agnosticism, therefore, claims that, regarding certain objects, among them the Deity, we can never have any positive empirical-scientific grounds either for belief or unbelief; and that, understood in this way, it should be clear that agnosticism does not entail atheism of either the negative or positive sort; and that the requirement of *demonstration* rather than *speculation* is even compatible with theism, provided of course that the believer can provide the necessary evidence for God's existence. But, being fair to Huxley, the expectation that such evidence will be forthcoming was for him extremely low, and explains why he himself rejected as the grossest forms of superstition the belief in miracles, the *Genesis* explanations of creation, biblical infallibility, divine providence and life after death. While these he regarded as insults to our intelligence, Huxley's principle required that no logical exclusion was intended here and that one must always remain open to conviction where evidence can be brought to establish the truth of such transcendent religious claims.[10]

With these various distinctions behind us – between positive and negative atheism and agnosticism – it should be stated from the outset that *The Atheist's Primer* is, for the most part, an exercise in positive atheism; and that accordingly I am here providing a survey of those arguments which assert that the claims of theistic religion are unjustified, and that valid grounds can be given for why this is. This is not to ignore negative atheism; but the difference between the two can be overworked. All atheism, of whatever stripe, is essentially negative in character in so far as it implies a lack of theistic belief: to that extent positive atheism is a form of negative atheism. But whereas in negative atheism the absence of belief in God results from unfamiliarity, in positive atheism it results from the rational demonstration that the central claims of theism – that, for example, there exists an all-good, all-powerful and all-knowing God – are invalid. Negative atheism, we might say, is positive atheism without the arguments; and it is these arguments that warrant the conclusion that no God exists. Hence the belief that theism has been, is or will be refuted is the core belief of the positive atheist's creed, the principal ambition being to expose the fact that religious belief has little intellectual support.

---

10 See 'Agnosticism' (1889), *Collected Essays*, Volume 5, London, Macmillan, 1894, pp.209-263. See also *TAC*: 33-38.

2
The Origins of Atheism

i. The Age of the Sophists

The origins of Western atheism lie in classical antiquity, in which first developed a naturalistic and empirical explanation of the world. Already visible in Greece in the philosophy of the Sophists of the second half of the fifth century B.C., this replacement of divine by natural causation became much more pronounced in the later schools of Epicurean Materialism and Scepticism. It is not easy to say precisely why this occurred, and why the old mythological conception of the gods as the sole agents of creation should have declined so rapidly. Various explanations have been offered. Gaskin suggests that the multiple polytheisms of the classical world led to considerable leeway in matters of religion, and that this, coupled with the lack of any unified priesthood, generated a 'tolerance concerning philosophical inquiry that resulted in lack of religion', provided only that this lack did not lead to an 'unpatriotic defamation of the gods'.[1] The reasons given by W.K. Guthrie are more extensive. Guthrie writes that the Greeks of this period developed a new intellectual latitude through increasing contact with other peoples, through war, travel and colonization; that their pride in their own technological achievements and material progress fostered a more practical understanding of the universe; that the growth of democracy at Athens inspired a much greater ideological flexibility; and that for these reasons the laws, customs and conventions of Greece – including, therefore, the conventions of religion – were no longer considered part of the immutable order of things but that different attitudes could be adopted towards them.[2]

This is not to say, however, that atheism during this period burgeoned as a popular movement. Positive atheism, as the specific denial of the existence of the gods, was a comparatively rare phenomenon, voiced by relatively few intellectuals, for the most part philosophers, and even they were extremely wary of challenging the accepted norms of a culture and society saturated

---

1   J.C.A. Gaskin (ed.,) *Varieties of Unbelief*, London, Collier Macmillan, 1989, p.6.
2   W.K.C. Guthrie, *The Sophists*, Cambridge, Cambridge University Press, 1971, pp.3-26.

with religious temples, rites, and festivals. And no wonder. Athenian criminal law employed the technical term *asebeia*, meaning impiety or disrespect towards the gods. At first the rule covered no more than offences against public worship, such as the felling of sacred trees or performing the wrong kind of sacrifice; but gradually the law was tightened to cover the rejection of accepted dogma, and by the late fifth and early fourth century B.C. a number of philosophers had been prosecuted, and even condemned, for denial of the gods. The list, as compiled by Drachmann,[3] includes most famously Socrates (469-399 B.C.) but also many of his Sophist contemporaries, and it is worth recording what some of them had to say. The earliest and most famous of the Sophists, Protagoras (c.490-420 B.C.), is distinguished as the first philosopher officially named an 'atheist' (*atheos*). The opening sentence of his *Concerning the Gods*, although in fact more agnostic than atheistic in tone, makes the accusation of impiety at least understandable. It reads: 'Concerning the gods I am unable to discover whether they exist or not, or what they are like in form; for there are many hindrances to knowledge, the obscurity of the subject and the brevity of human life'.[4] Another accused is Diagoras of Melos, a legendary figure of this period about whom next to nothing is known, except that he always appears as 'the atheist', a title earned for ridiculing and divulging the Eleusinian Mysteries. More justifiably denounced was Prodicus of Keos (c.465-395 B.C.), who held that the gods were named after those products of the earth which benefited humanity – hence bread was associated with Demeter, wine with Dionysus, water with Poseidon, fire with Hephaestus – and thus presents one of the earliest anthropological theories about the purely human origin of the gods. The political aristocrat Critias (c.450-403 B.C.), a reactionary member of the Thirty Tyrants, who seized power at the end of the Peloponnesian War, is classified as *atheos* solely on the strength of the play *Sisyphus* attributed to him. He writes:

> Once there was a time when the life of human beings was disordered, and similar to that of animals and ruled by force, when there was no reward for the virtuous nor any punishment for the wicked. And then I think that humans decided to establish laws as punishers so that Justice (*Dikē*) might be ruler . . . and keep Crime and Violence (*Hybris*) as slave. And they punished only those who kept doing wrong. Then, since the laws held open deeds of violence in check, they continued to commit them in secret; then, I believe, a wise and clever-minded man invented for mortals a fear of the gods, so that there might be a deterrent for the wicked,

---

3   A.B. Drachmann, *Atheism in Pagan Antiquity*, London, Gyldendal, 1922, p.13.
4   Quoted by Guthrie, *Op.cit.*, p.234.

even if they act or say or think anything in secret. Hence from this source he explained the divine: there is a deity (*daimôn*) who enjoys imperishable life, hearing and seeing with his mind, his thought and attention on all things, bearer of a divine nature. He will hear whatever is said among mortals and be able to see whatever is done. If you silently plot evil, this will not escape the gods. For they . . . have knowledge. With these words he explained the most delightful part of the teaching and hid the truth with a false tale. He said the gods dwell there where he – by placing them there – could frighten human beings most, whence, as he knew, fears come to mortals and troubles for their wretched life; that is, from the vault on high, where they beheld the lightnings and fearful blows of thunder and heaven with its starry eyes, the beautiful, brilliantly decorated building of Time, the wise craftsman. Whence too the brilliant mass of the sun strides and the liquid rain falls on the earth. . . . It was thus, I think, that someone first persuaded mortals to believe that there exists a race of gods.[5]

This passage, famous in the history of atheism, is the first presentation of the theory that religion is a deliberate invention by governments to ensure the good behaviour of its subjects, and could sit, without embarrassment, within the pages of Sigmund Freud's *The Future of an Illusion*, written twenty-four centuries later.

The trial and execution of Socrates for *asabeia* proved a watershed in the legal indictment of philosophers for denying the gods, and thereafter a more pragmatic tolerance took hold: one could hold atheistic beliefs and one need not participate in the worship of the deities; but as soon as these practical refusals converted into public denunciations of the established religion and morality, they were regarded as dangerous political and social activities and such civic disloyalty was treated with the utmost severity. For this reason, Socrates' pupil, Plato (427-347 B.C.), himself a conservative theist and so deploring the 'malady of atheism', distinguishes between two types of atheist: one capable of leading a moral life and posing no threat to society, the other immoral and devious, and to be restrained by punishment and imprisonment.[6]

The age of the Sophists includes one other important figure to mention, not himself a member of that group but nevertheless crucial for the later development of atheistic thought in classical antiquity:

---

5   Quoted by Jan N. Bremmer, 'Atheism in Antiquity,' *The Cambridge Companion to Atheism*, ed. Michael Martin, Cambridge, Cambridge University Press, 2007, p.17.

6   *The Laws*, 908b-e. *Plato: The Collected Dialogues*, translated by A.E. Taylor, and edited by Edith Hamilton and Huntington Cairns, New York, Bollingen Foundation, 1966, pp.1463-1464.

Democritus

Democritus of Abdera (c.460-400 B.C.), the greatest of the Greek physical philosophers, and recorded as a fellow-townsman and mentor of Protagoras. With his teacher, Leucippus, Democritus is the co-founder of the theory of Atomism. This theory explains the phenomena of the universe through the constant motion within infinite space (or the Void) of an infinite number of eternal, invisible and uncaused atoms (*atomoi*). The visible world is the result of the constant rearrangement into different forms and shapes of these indestructible atoms, and however varied their perceived forms may appear to the senses, they are in fact no more than compounds of the same timeless atoms. As Democritus remarks, 'A thing is only hot or cold, sweet or bitter, by convention; the only things that exist in reality are the atoms and the void'. Thus nothing can come into being or perish, matter and motion are eternal, and the origins of the universe can be explained according to a purely mechanical system, with its own fixed and necessary laws. This eliminated any idea of providence or purposive creation by an intelligent deity. How, then, are we to explain the popular idea of the gods? The tenor of Democritus' system is anti-theistic: he attributed religious belief to the need to explain the extraordinary and frightening phenomena of the natural world – e.g., thunder, lightning, comets and eclipses – by reference to some superhuman agency; but he yielded to popular prejudice insofar as he conceded that there did exist certain beings, mortal but composed of subtler atoms and thus less liable to extinction, dwelling in a twilight realm within the upper regions of the air, and who manifested themselves in the images (*eidola*) of men's dreams.

While Democritus and the Sophists may have retained a residual belief in divine forces, more pantheistic than atheistic, they developed ideas on religion far removed from the anthropomorphic divinities of the Olympian pantheon, which continued to flourish; but so long as the gods of popular worship were regarded as powerful cohesive factors, integral to the life of the state, these philosophers adopted a cautious attitude of critical tolerance towards them, accepting the existing cultic practices only with strict reservations. However, these reservations were to increase in tandem with the continuing development of materialist inter- pretations of the mechanisms of nature. For these interpretations, if not completely atheistic, by offering explanations of the world and its contents framed solely within the dynamic processes of nature itself, left little room for teleology and the deification of causal forces.

Epicurus

ii. Epicureans and Sceptics

The intellectual ambivalence towards religion expressed by the Sophists is equally apparent in the philosophical movement that followed them, and which for our purposes is of still greater importance, not least because of the extent and durability of the movement's influence, which helped proselytize an anti-teleological physics throughout the ancient world. This is the school of Epicurean Materialism. Its founder, Epicurus of Samos (341-270 B.C.), freely acknowledges that the atomic theory he presents owes much to Democritus, although admittedly here overhauled and extended to such a degree as to be considered original by his contemporaries. So, in his *Letter to Herodotus* Epicurus covers the familiar Democritean ground, and expatiates on the eternal motions of the indissoluble atoms within the infinities of space or the 'Void', this constant movement forever replacing one world with another. Such a materialist system is atheistic in all but name. Epicurus, like Democritus before him, never specifically denies the gods of traditional religion; but these beings are themselves no more than products of the natural order, to be regarded as eternal idealizations of moral perfection and so deserving of worship, but nonetheless material like everything else and so incapable of controlling or interfering in human destiny. This freedom from the gods releases man from the superstitions of religion – most notably from the fear of what happens after death – and allows for the development of a habit of mind characterized by *ataraxia* or *apatheia*: by imperturbability and mental tranquillity.[7]

---

7 See *TAC*: 57-63

It is interesting to note that it is this relegation of the gods, not the denial of their existence, which later defined Epicureans as 'practical atheists' and explains their contemptuous rejection of Paul the Apostle at Athens in A.D. 50/51 and his teaching on divine providence and the resurrection of the dead (*Acts* 17:18). Karl Marx (1818-1883), who wrote his doctoral dissertation on Democritus and Epicurus (1841), acknowledges Epicurus' influence as follows:

> Epicurus . . . was the true radical Enlightener of antiquity; he openly attacked the ancient religion, and it was from him, too, that the atheism of the Romans, insofar as it existed, was derived. For this reason, too, Lucretius praised Epicurus as the hero who was the first to overthrow the gods and trample religion underfoot; for this reason among all church fathers, from Plutarch to Luther, Epicurus has always had the reputation of being the atheist philosopher *par excellence*, and was called a swine; for which reason, too, Clement of Alexandria says that when Paul takes up arms against philosophy he has in mind Epicurean philosophy alone.[8]

For Epicurus, then, religion operates for the most part as a hindrance to moral development and the overriding epicurean concern to seek happiness and avoid pain. This conclusion, despite attempts by its detractors to present the theory as no more than a license for sensual pleasure, proved enormously popular, not merely in Greece but in Asia and Egypt, and by about 150 B.C. Epicureanism had established itself in Rome. Here the leading exponent of Epicureanism was the poet Lucretius, whose *De Rerum Natura* – the greatest poem to embody great philosophy and written in the epic style of Homer – sets out the main teaching of Epicurus with great precision: if there are gods, they are unconcerned with humanity and incapable of affecting the natural world.[9] The poem is divided into six books, but the third deserves special

---

8   Marx-Engels, *The German Ideology*, Chapter Three, Section 'The Ancients'. Text available at www.marxists.org.

9   It is also worth recording what Lucretius has to say about Epicurus: 'When human life lay grovelling in all men's sight, crushed to the earth under the dead weight of superstition whose grim features loured menacingly upon mortals from the four quarters of the sky, a man of Greece was the first to raise mortal eyes in defiance, first to stand erect and brave the challenge. Fables of the gods did not crush him, nor the lightning flash and the growing menace of the sky. Rather they quickened his manhood, so that he, first of all men, longed to smash the constraining locks of nature's doors. The vital vigour of his mind prevailed. He ventured far out beyond the flaming ramparts of the world and voyaged in mind throughout infinity. Returning victorious, he proclaimed to us what can be and what cannot: how a limit is

mention. This contains Lucretius'
famous account of the nature of
the mind, which shows that the soul
perishes with the body and that fear
of death is therefore unwarranted.

Lucretius

> And since the mind is one part
> of a man which remains fixed
> in a particular spot, just as are
> the ears and eyes and the other
> senses which guide and direct
> life; and just as the hand or eye
> or nose when separated from us
> cannot feel and exist apart, but
> in a very short time wastes away
> in putrefaction, thus the mind
> cannot exist by itself without the
> body and the man himself, which as you see serves for the mind's
> vessel or anything else you choose to imagine which implies a
> yet closer union with it, since the body is attached to it by the
> closest ties. . . . Death is therefore nothing to us, concerns us not
> a jot, since the nature of the mind is proved to be mortal; . . .
> thus when we shall be no more, when there shall have been a
> separation of body and soul, out of both of which we are each
> formed into a single being, to us, you may be sure, who then shall
> be no more, nothing whatever can happen to excite sensation,
> not if earth were to be mingled with sea and sea with heaven.
> And even supposing the nature of the mind and power of the
> soul do feel, after they have been severed from our body, yet
> that is nothing to us who by the binding tie of marriage between
> body and soul are formed each into one single being. And if time
> should gather up our matter after our death and put it once more
> into the position in which it now is, and the light of life be given
> to us again, even this result would concern us not at all, when the
> chain of our self-consciousness has once been snapped asunder.
> So now we give ourselves no concern about any self which we
> have been before, nor do we feel any distress on the score of
> that self. For when you look back on the whole past course of
> immeasurable time and think how manifold are the shapes which

---

fixed to the power of everything and an immovable frontier post. Therefore,
superstition in its turn lies crushed beneath his feet, and we by his triumph
are lifted level with the skies'. *On the Nature of the Universe*, trans. R.E. Latham,
Harmondsworth, Penguin, 1951, p.29.

the motions of matter take, you may easily believe that these very same seeds of which we now are formed have often before been placed in the same order in which they now are; and yet we cannot recover this in memory: a break in our existence has been interposed, and all the motions have wandered to and fro astray from the sensations they produce. For he upon whom evil is to befall must in his own person exist at the very time it comes, if the misery and suffering are by chance to have any place at all; but since death precludes this, and forbids him to be, upon whom the ills can be brought, you may be sure that we have nothing to fear after death, and that he who does not exist cannot become miserable, and that it matters not a whit whether he has been born into life at any other time, when immortal death has taken away his mortal life.[10]

As we have seen, the Epicurean position on religion derives from a specific theory of reality. This stressed the infinite variety and eternality of matter and so excluded any notion of an ultimate cause or transcendent deity intervening in the processes of existence. Gods there may be but not of a kind to order nature to their own design. It was, however, left to the last of the so-called Greek schools – the school of Scepticism – to maintain this exclusion in a still more radical fashion. Almost all that we know about Scepticism – or Pyrrhonism, as it was called until the end of the nineteenth century, after its founder, Pyrrho of Elis (c.365-275 B.C.) – depends on the detailed accounts given by Sextus Empiricus. Little is known of Sextus, except that he was a doctor – his Latin name *empiricus* possibly referring to his membership of a particular school of medicine – and that he was almost certainly Greek, living some time during the latter half of the second century A.D. As Sextus makes clear, the exclusion of the gods by the Sceptics was not made on the basis of any epicurean claim to a knowledge in physics: it was made, rather, on more general epistemological grounds, that regarded all such claims to objective knowledge, of whatever hue, as 'dogmatic' and unjustified, including therefore both knowledge of the gods and the natural world. Thus, while the intention of the Sceptics was similarly to attain peace of mind or *ataraxia*, they differed from their predecessors in how this was to be achieved. For the Epicureans, to repeat, it could be reached by accepting that the universe is a vast self-creating mechanism impervious to divine interference; but for the Sceptics it could be obtained only by realizing that there is no conclusive evidence one way or the other for *any* of the beliefs by which men live – to suppose that there is only leads to an unnecessary expenditure of energy and inevitable

---

10 *TAC*: 66-68

disappointment. Admittedly the Sceptics differed among themselves in respect to the degree and the extent of their scepticism. Some, the so-called Academic Sceptics, produced arguments claiming that no certain knowledge was possible; but for others, the so-called Pyrrhonian Sceptics, even this conclusion was suspicious and asserted too much: they argued instead that judgment should be withheld on all questions about which there seemed to be conflicting

Carneades

evidence, including therefore the question whether or not something could be known. Needless to say, the universal doubt employed here to achieve peace of mind leads directly to an agnosticism that offers no support for either theistic or atheistic belief. For according to the principle of suspending judgement (*epoche*), atheism was also a dogmatic belief to be deplored equally with its antithesis. This meant that the Sceptics were very far from supporting positive disbelief in the gods and were largely content, like the philosophers of earlier times, to make public concessions to the popular faith, to offer proper worship and reverence, even though what they professed in private was very different.

This certainly was the position taken by Pyrrho and his immediate successors; but by the time we get to the celebrated sceptic and logician Carneades of Cyrene (c.214-129 B.C.), who took over the headship of Plato's Academy in 167, a much more critical and less generous approach towards religion had emerged. Carneades holds to the familiar line of suspending judgment, and is accordingly not even sure that he can be sure of nothing; but this absence of any criterion of truth does not prevent him from launching a withering attack upon theistic assumptions. First Carneades attacks the argument, later known as the *argumentum e consensu gentium* or argument from the general consent of mankind, that claimed the universality of religious belief was evidence of the truth of religious belief – an argument dismissed by Carneades as of anthropological or sociological interest only but of absolutely no logical weight: that a belief is true is not confirmed by how many people believe it. Nor can any credence be attached to the doctrine of a divinely ordained providence. For not only is there no proof to suggest that the world is anything but the product of natural forces, but even within the world there are elements which both count against beneficent design, like poisonous snakes and disease, and count for accidental design, like the rock formed into a head-shape, this invalidating the argument that design implies designer. And finally, Carneades attacks the idea of God itself, pointing to contradictions within the divine attributes. To take two:

1 Either God has or has not a body; but if he is incorporeal he is inanimate and so without senses and incapable of thought or activity; but if he is corporeal he is subject to change and so perishable. There being no further alternative, we must conclude that God is therefore neither incorporeal nor corporeal, that indeed God is nothing, and so does not exist.
2 God is an all-virtuous being. To be virtuous, however, God must overcome dangers and pains. But pains and dangers only exist for a being who can suffer or be destroyed by them. Since, therefore, the qualities of suffering and destructibility are incompatible with the notion of a perfect being, no such being exists.

According to Douglas Walton, the dialectical power of these arguments 'reveal the stature of Carneades as a skeptical philosopher'; and interestingly enough Walton then proceeds to construct a formal disproof of the existence of God based on them.[11]

It is a measure of the religious tolerance during the second century B.C. that Carneades, who in earlier times would almost certainly have been convicted of *asebeia*, was entrusted with important diplomatic missions on behalf of the State, the most notable being his embassy to Rome in 155 B.C. to protest against a fine imposed upon Athens. But, while there, it is noteworthy that it was not his attitude to religion that attracted attention so much as his ability to argue on both sides of a case. In a celebrated demonstration of dialectical skill, on one day Carneades argued in favour of justice and on the next against it – a tour de force that created huge excitement among the young intellectuals of Rome. And this degree of tolerance was by no means unusual. Romans only gradually acquired the Greek taste for philosophy, and with the rapid expansion of the Empire had, of necessity, taken a much more pragmatic attitude towards those of different faiths. It is only with the advent of the two monotheistic religions of the East – Judaism and Christianity – that active steps were taken by the authorities to crush religious dissent, and this was done because these faiths offered a practical, rather than

---

11 'Can an ancient argument of Carneades on cardinal virtues and divine attributes be used to disprove the existence of God?' *The Impossibility of God*, ed. Michael Martin and Ricki Monnier, Amherst, New York, Prometheus Books, 2003, pp.35-44.

merely theoretical, denial of the
gods, which struck at the heart of
Roman society.

This difference between a public and private attitude towards
the gods is best illustrated in the life
and work of the Roman statesman
and orator, Marcus Tullius Cicero
(106-43 B.C.). As an active
politician Cicero fully endorses the
religious orthodoxy of his time,
and in his *De Legibus* underscores
the necessity of an established
religion, in which the customs,
festivals, rites and prayers of the
sacra publica operate as safeguards

Cicero

of social stability and constitutional order. But if public acceptance was one
thing, private endorsement was quite another. For a man of learning such
as Cicero personal religion meant philosophical speculation, and it was to
philosophy that he turned as a guide on all the major questions of life. As
a creative philosopher Cicero is unimportant; but as a prolific compiler and
translator into Latin of philosophical ideas he has no equal, introducing
his Roman readers almost for the first time to the central themes of Greek
thought. His dialogue *De Natura Deorum*, written in the last years of his
life, clearly reveals his sympathies, applying the criticisms of the Sceptics,
and of Carneades in particular, almost wholesale to the claims of theistic
belief. And once again the familiar themes are rehearsed: if there are gods,
they are indifferent to us; to believe in them is not a requirement of the
moral life; and fortune is capricious rather than earned. Human beings
stand, therefore, as the arbiters of their own destinies. These views were
not uncommon, and in all Cicero's copious correspondence there is no
suggestion that any of his upper class friends found them blasphemous.

To conclude: in the classical world we find the beginnings of a
naturalistic account of the world and of man's place within it devoid of
any theistic overlay. Despite the later policy of the Emperor Augustus
(63 B.C.-A.D. 14) to restore the old deities of Rome to pre-eminence
in public life, and his construction of new temples to the deified Julius
Caesar, to Mars the Avenger or to his own special patron, Apollo, these
remained expressions of popular not private belief, glorifications of the
State and manifestations of a new public confidence after years of civil
strife. But the agnostic tradition, often tantamount to atheism, remained
a functioning alternative, visible in the literature of the Augustan elite: we

find it, for example, in the Epicurean pessimism of the Epistles of Horace (65-8 B.C), in the posthumous poems of Rome's greatest writer, Virgil (70-19 B.C.) – both authors being recipients of Augustus' patronage – and in the cynical irreverence towards the old gods in the poetry of Ovid (43 B.C.-A.D. 17). One of the most significant pronouncements is to be found in the encyclopaedic *Naturalis Historia* of Pliny the Elder (A.D. 23-79). The 'folly' of believing in the Roman pantheon can be easily exposed: it derives, to follow Democritus, from the deification of natural phenomena, from the personification of the virtue and vices of man, of what men seek and desire. And within the pantheistic identification that Pliny offers between God and the universe, there is no place for Providence:

> But it agrees with life's experience to believe that in these matters the gods exercise an interest in human affairs; and that punishment for wickedness, though sometimes tardy, as God is occupied in so vast a mass of things, yet is never frustrated; and that man was not born God's next of kin for the purpose of approximating to the beasts in vileness. But the chief consolations for nature's imperfection in the case of man are that not even for God are all things possible – for he cannot, even if he wishes, commit suicide, the supreme boon that he has bestowed on man among all the penalties of life, nor bestow eternity on mortals or recall the deceased, nor cause a man that has lived not to have lived or one that has held high office not to have held it – and that he has no power over what is past save to forget it, and (to link our fellowship with God by means of frivolous arguments as well) that he cannot cause twice ten not to be twenty or do many things on similar lines: which facts unquestionably demonstrate the power of nature, and prove that it is this that we mean by the word 'God'.[12]

iii. The Christian Era and the Re-emergence of Religious Doubt

That such views could be uttered without official censure is evidence of the remarkable intellectual latitude of the Augustan age, but only so long as such beliefs were speculative in form and not practical in operation. But with the emergence of Christianity as the dominant religion of the western world, and its accession to political power under the Emperor Constantine (A.D. 280-337), such toleration came to a rapid end, and such freethinking alternatives were repressed with an ideological ferocity unknown in classical antiquity.[13] The exclusivism of a monotheistic dogma, which lay claim to

---

12 *Natural History*, translated H. Rackham, Loeb Classical Library, London, William Heinemann, 1958, Vol.1, pp.185-187.

13 Edward Gibbon makes clear that the Roman persecutions of the early

a unique revelation – the incarnation of Jesus Christ as the one true God – left little room, under the mandate of apostolic authority, for philosophical manoeuvre: 'If any one is preaching to you a gospel contrary to that which you have received', writes Paul the Apostle, 'let him be accursed'.[14] This demand for unquestioning allegiance, when backed up by a succession of theocratic governments always quick to sniff out and deal mercilessly with heresy, effectively silenced any discussion of alternatives. In 529 the

Giordano Bruno

Christian Emperor Justinian closed the Athenian school of philosophy, the Academy, which had existed since the time of Plato; and under Gregory the Great (590-604), the first Pope to establish his authority over the entire Roman Church, a deliberate policy was introduced to destroy all surviving pagan books, temples and statuary.

It is therefore a lamentable but entirely understandable fact that no significant agnostic or atheistic literature now appears until the late sixteenth and early seventeenth centuries, that is, until the publications of Giordano Bruno (1548-1600) and Giulio Vanini (1585-1619). However, the fact that both men were burnt at the stake as heretics provides a salutary reminder, if ever one was needed, of the dangers of introducing a worldview contrary to the dominant teaching of the Church – in Bruno's case, a pantheistic cosmology in which a personal God is replaced by an immanent deity identified with a plurality of worlds constantly evolving within a dynamic and infinite universe. Nor can it be regarded as entirely fortuitous that the re-emergence of religious doubt during this period coincides with the rediscovery of the writers of the classical world. Bruno's cosmic vision of innumerable worlds is indebted

---

Christians, even under Diocletian, were as nothing compared to the later horrors perpetrated by the Christians upon themselves. In the controversial Chapters 15 and 16 of his *History of the Decline and Fall of the Roman Empire* (published in six volumes, 1776-1788) and speaking of the policy of Charles V in the Netherlands, which accounted for over one hundred thousand deaths, he writes: 'If we are obliged to submit our belief to the authority of Grotius, it must be allowed that the number of Protestants who were executed in a single province and a single reign far exceeded that of the primitive martyrs in the space of three centuries and of the Roman empire.' Quoted from the abridged edition by D.M. Low, London, The Reprint Society, 1960, p. 238.

14 *Galations*. 1:8-9

Sextus Empiricus

to his reading of Epicurus and Lucretius; but the most notable discovery of the time was of Sextus Empiricus: first published in 1562, by the end of the seventeenth century he had been transformed into 'the divin Sexte'. Michel de Montaigne (1533-1592), the most significant figure in the revival of scepticism in the sixteenth century, had the sayings of Sextus carved into the rafters of his study; and his *Apologie de Raimond Sebond* (1576) – with its famous motto, 'Que sais-je?' (What do I know?) – is his own attempt to deal with the intellectual crisis of knowledge if, following Sextus, everything is to be doubted. For Pierre Bayle (1647-1706), perhaps the most important sceptic of the seventeenth century, Sextus was no less than the father of modern philosophy. Bayle's *Dictionnaire historique et critique* (1697) provided detailed biographies of Sextus and other sceptics and provided Bayle himself with a platform from which to expose the irrationalities of religious belief, to argue that no good and omnipotent God could have created an evil world, and that atheists could be more moral than Christians. While scholars may still debate about Bayle's own religious beliefs, the impact of his views is undoubted. The *Dictionnaire*, called by Voltaire 'the Arsenal of the Enlightenment', went through several editions in the eighteenth century and was a major influence on the re-fashioned scepticism of David Hume (1711-1776). Indeed, in Hume – the greatest philosopher ever to write in English – the sceptical tradition inherited from Carneades and Sextus, and the naturalistic tradition descending from Epicurus and Lucretius, reach their culmination. Against the three specific arguments supporting what he calls 'the religious hypothesis' – the Cosmological Argument, the Argument from Design and the Argument from Miracles – Hume's scepticism is deployed to devastating effect. Two of these arguments will be discussed in the next chapter; but for the moment it is sufficient to say that together they provide what is generally considered the most sustained and influential attack ever mounted against theistic rationality. To that extent, Hume stands as the philosophic heir of the sceptical and naturalist teachings of the classical world.

3
Two Arguments for God's Existence:
An Atheistic Critique

i. Introduction

For the positive atheist's case to succeed, a range of classic arguments for God's existence must be refuted.[1] Although sometimes called 'proofs', only one of them can lay legitimate claim to that name. This is the so-called ontological argument first presented by Anselm of Canterbury (c.1033-1109). Here Anselm argues that, from the definition of God – that 'God is something than which nothing greater can be conceived' – one may conclude, as a matter of logic, that God exists, his existence

Anselm of Canterbury

being a necessary requirement of his unsurpassable greatness. The *a priori* character of this argument – which involves no appeal to experience and so no experiential evidence to determine truth or falsity – makes it unique in the history of theology. But, although undoubtedly of great philosophical interest, and despite having modern advocates, this argument is for the most part rejected by philosophers on lines first drawn by Immanuel Kant in his *Critique of Pure Reason* of 1791. We may allow that the concept of God as the greatest conceivable and most perfect being is correct; but this does not imply that the concept is instantiated anywhere in existence. Nothing, in other words, can be defined into existence. From the definition of X, it does not follow that X exists.

We can therefore set the ontological argument to one side. However, other classic arguments remain, and it is these, often generally classified as cosmological in character (from the Greek *cosmos*, meaning 'universe'

---

1 These are analysed in much greater detail in my *The Question of God: An Introduction and Sourcebook*, London, Routledge, 2001. Hereafter cited as *QG*.

or 'world'), which are among the primary targets of the atheistic literature. From the evidence drawn from certain empirical observations or experiences of the world about us, it is concluded that God exists, this being the only rational explanation sufficient to explain what has occurred. These observations and experiences can range from the familiar – that, for example, things exist, move, are caused, and exhibit some degree of order – to the unfamiliar: that certain individuals have witnessed or themselves experienced events so extraordinary that they call them 'miraculous'. Such arguments have also been called 'proofs'; but, strictly speaking, proofs they are not. For these arguments are not *a priori* in form but *a posteriori* in character, and as such always allow for the possibility, however remote, of falsifying evidence becoming available. These, then, are not proofs in the Anselmic sense by claiming that the denial of God's existence is self-contradictory, but proofs only in the sense that they assert that such a denial is unreasonable, given the weight of evidence against it. As with all *a posteriori* arguments, what is being claimed here is not, then, that these theistic explanations are the only *logically possible* explanations but rather that they are the only *plausible* explanations of the available evidence, and that these can be presented beyond rational doubt. Two of these arguments are of particular merit. These are the famous arguments from Cause and Design.

ii. The Arguments from Cause and Design

It will come as no surprise that many of the fiercest critics of these arguments refer back to those authors of classical Greece who offered an interpretation of the universe, and of man's place within it, devoid of any theistic concepts of order and design. For in a scheme that claimed that the cosmos was of infinite extent and duration, no place could be found for an initial beginning inaugurated and supervised by an interventionist deity; and in a programme of creation marked by its atomistic randomness, any notion of a designing intelligence could be excluded. For the most part, however, these ideas, which, we recall, first took shape in the fifth century B.C., were exclusive to the philosophical community; but even here, as we noted, public confessions of explicit atheism were virtually unknown and played no part in popular religion. For the general public, while the domestic wranglings of the mythic gods of Olympus may have appeared increasingly ridiculous, the faith in a supra-natural world, peopled by superior beings, remained intact, and the formalities of the cult continued to celebrate the belief that the formation of the world and the visible regularities of nature within it were explicable in terms of the divine decrees of the gods, a frequent analogy being drawn between divine commands and the edicts of a lawgiver.

Despite, therefore, the presence of mechanistic explanations, the idea of divine causation and design was never completely eliminated from Greek speculation. It is, however, with Plato (427-347 B.C.) that this supernaturalist view finds its first formal justification, with a detailed philosophical rejection of the claim that the sequence of natural events occurs mechanically and is indifferent to purpose. In Plato's dialogue the *Laws*, we meet the first exposition of the famous 'First Cause' argument, developed to offset the possibility

Plato

of an infinite regress of causes; and then, in the dialogue *Timaeus*, a design argument repudiating any notion of a self-explanatory and self-generating universe, and in which the universe is symbolically presented as a 'living creature', ordered and intelligent, and fashioned by a benevolent craftsman or Demiurge. However, a significantly different picture emerges with Plato's most celebrated pupil, Aristotle (384-322 B.C.). For while Aristotle shares with his teacher a keen sense of the philosophical necessity of a supreme causal principle, which he names the Unmoved Mover, he rejects altogether the Platonic teleological addition. As he explains in Book 12 of the *Metaphysics*, God is the eternal unchanging source of all change, movement and process – the ultimate mover that guides intermediate movers (i.e., humans) – but while thus indispensable to the world's existence, this supreme mover of the universe is not a creator-god: first, because the universe is itself eternal, an ordered world of natural processes without beginning or end, in everlasting and continuous motion; and second, because a perfect being has no needs and can do nothing to improve its state. Aristotle's Unmoved Mover thus stands aloof from the universe as an immutable perfection, the apex of all being and knowledge, but as a deity unaware of the world and so caring nothing for it, without any desire to create or act within something less perfect than itself. The unbroken activity of God is thus directed not outwards in intervening providential acts of design but solely inwards, in an introspective activity of contemplation. Here the Unmoved Mover

Aristotle

focuses upon the only object adequate to exercise his thoughts, namely, Himself.

While after Aristotle there were sporadic revivals of naturalistic interpretations of creation – Lucretius and Cicero, we remember, were both advocates of this view – none of these was sufficiently powerful to challenge the prevailing theistic idea, now reinforced by the intellectual ascendancy of the Platonic and Aristotelian philosophies. However, with the advent of Christianity as the dom-inant European belief-system, both the old gods and any pantheistic or atheistic alternatives were totally eclipsed, and indeed vigorously repressed. Christian monotheism proclaimed an omnipotent, omniscient and personal deity, much given to divine interventions in the affairs of mortals as the merciful and providential father of his children. And an essential part of this outlook, adopted from the Jewish tradition, was enshrined in the biblical myth of creation. The world was brought into being 'from nothing' (*ex nihilo*) within a specified time-frame by an all-powerful God, who engineered its completion in scrupulous detail, giving to all creatures their proper place and function. This process culminates in the creation of man, made in the image of God (*imago dei*) – this likeness to God giving to human beings a central role in the cosmic drama thereafter to be played out according to the divine plan.

In its bare essentials, it is this scheme of divine causation and design which now dominates the intellectual landscape until the seventeenth century. Christian doctrine confirmed that the universe as a whole had been planned on a grand scale, a divine design no less, and that it was part of God's purpose that the creation he had caused to be should also tend towards some aim or end (*telos*). The root idea took hold that, given that the actions of human agents were observed to have some purpose, the universe could, by analogy, be viewed in the same way, the even greater complexity and orderliness of the universe pointing to a conscious agent infinitely greater than any human counterpart. Christian theology, however, had to wait until the thirteenth century – that is, until

the work of Thomas Aquinas
(1225-1274) – for the full
expression of these ideas,
presented, we should add,
at a level of philosophical
sophistication fully the equal
of that achieved by either
Plato or Aristotle.

Aquinas' arguments from
cause and design appear as the
second and fifth proofs of his
famous 'Five Ways' (*quinque
viae*) in his *Summa Theologiae*,
begun in 1256 but unfinished
at his death. For our purposes
all we need say is that in
each case Aquinas offers a

Thomas Aquinas

theistic explanation of reality that is, he maintains, the only plausible
explanation of why things are as they are. So, in the causal argument,
the possibility of an infinite regression of causes and their effects, of
the kind proposed in the atomic theories of a Democritus, is rejected
on the grounds that, while our immediate experience may explain why
any particular effect has a particular cause, an infinite series of regressive
causes does not explain why anything should exist in the first place. All
it offers is an explanation of cause and effect in terms of other causes
and other effects, leaving us to suppose, improbably enough, that things
owe their existence to nothing but themselves. A theistic explanation,
on the other hand, offers no such implausibility. For just as in everyday
experience we assume that any particular thing (the effect X) exists by
virtue of another thing (the cause Y), and agree that this relation offers
a justified explanation of why X exists, so the existence of God, as the
First Cause, offers a justified explanation of why the world as a whole
exists, why it came into existence, and why it continues to exist. That
there is something and not nothing can be explained, in other words,
through the permanent and present power of God, with the converse
truth that without his continuing and sustaining existence nothing would
now exist.

Let us turn now to the design argument. For the most celebrated
account we must move from the thirteenth century to the eighteenth
century, from Aquinas to William Paley (1743-1805), Archdeacon of
Carlisle. In his *Natural Theology* of 1802 Paley introduces his famous
(or notorious) comparison between the universe and a watch. Paley's

argument is simplicity itself. A watch is compared to a stone; and while we can imagine a stone evolving through chance factors like the wind or rain, the complexity of the watch makes it absurd to assume that it too came into existence through a set of random occurrences. So we conclude that some intelligence has been at work to create the watch. Paley then extends his argument to the universe generally and to particular natural objects within it, noting particularly that miracle of creation, the vertebrate eye, the examination of which is virtually a cure for atheism. Such wonderful intricacy, Paley concludes, by surpassing anything that the human mind could create, implies the presence of a mind which, by the same token, far surpasses any human intelligence; and it is this supra-human intelligence which must have been employed not just in the construction of the eye but in the creation of all that is.

It is worth unpacking this legendary argument a little further. In structure it is an *inductive argument from resemblances*. First a remarkable similarity is established between artifacts and organisms in that both adapt their means to ends: in the case of the watch, the movement of its interior mechanisms operating to measure hours; and in the case of the natural world, to give only one example, the movement of the earth round the sun accounting for the passage from night to day. Next, both artifacts and organisms are treated as *effects*; the similarity already established between them sanctioning the conclusion that *their causes must also be similar*. This is the crucial move in the argument and brings us to its most important presupposition. This is that there is a fundamental *order of things* to be discerned in every part of the universe, so that the structure of a certain part, such as belongs to organisms, can be inferred from the structure of another part, such as belongs to artifacts. It is this assumption of a *uniformity of nature* that is implied in every case of induction. We observe A followed by B not once, not twice, but a hundred times, and may thus safely predict that the next time we see A we shall also see B. In this sense we assume that nature is repetitious – that the sun will rise tomorrow because it rose today – and, on the basis of these recurring regularities, we formulate certain laws regarding future states of affairs: that arsenic is poisonous, that fire warms, that all men die, and so on.

This assumption of inductive uniformity allows Paley to claim that *like effects have like causes*. If we have variously observed a connection between the effect B (e.g., machines) and the cause A (e.g., mechanics), then by analogy when we meet a new instance of B we may infer that it too must have had a cause A. Here the regularity of nature is presumed not merely in our observation that all machines require mechanics but also in our further assumption that, when we see a new machine, *the creation of*

that we cannot directly observe,
we may infer by analogy
that here too a mechanic
has been at work. Once
again a uniformity of
nature is presumed. The
resemblance between things
like machines and the
universe entitles us to
infer by analogy that the
universe, like machines,
also has a mechanic,
even though the universe-
making of this particular
mechanic similarly *cannot
be directly observed.*

It should be underlined
again that, as an *a posteriori*

William Paley

cosmological proof, the design argument, like its causal counterpart,
makes no claims to be an *a priori* logical truth. Thus, however many
machines we have observed to have mechanics, and however certain we
may be that all future machines will have mechanics, we must allow that
the particular machine now under examination did not have a mechanic.
All we can say is that it most probably had one. But the fact that this
argument is not a logical proof is not seen by advocates as a weakness but
as a strength, placing it fully in line with the problematic and contingent
character of all empirical observations. Here, then, we are dealing with
probabilities and not with logical certainties. Their claim is rather that
the uniformity of nature observed within our world is such that it is
as probable that the world has a designer as it is that any machine we
come across has a mechanic. And the more instances we can call upon to
reinforce this understanding of machines, the more likely becomes our
interpretation of the world's origin. These instances are almost infinitely
numerous. Thus to deny that the world has a designer is to deny the
cumulative evidence of our senses.

iii. The Atheistic Critique

The authors of these two theistic arguments are claiming that the causal
laws and regularities in nature are more plausibly explained metaphysically,
with God as both the sustaining power and architect of all that is; and
that the alternative of an atheistic naturalism, according to which the
world explains itself, has in effect no persuasive power because, after

all, an explanation is no explanation if a further explanation is required
to explain it. What the arguments from Cause and Design offer, in
other words, are alternatives that appear ultimate, providing a terminus
of explanation that is incapable of further analysis. The cosmological
explanation designates God as the ultimate cause outside the universe –
eternal, imperishable and independent – and thus immune to the finite
constraints and perishabilities of that universe; and the teleological
explanation sees God as the ultimate designer, purposive and creative,
without whom the order and complexity of the universe would remain
inexplicable.

As a first step in the presentation of the positive atheist's case, it is
worth making the following general point. The theistic view, to repeat,
is that any fact X will be rendered unintelligible when divorced from an
account of how X came about; and that this is true whether the X here
stands for the fact that the world exists at all, as in the causal argument,
or for the fact that it exists in a certain way, as in the design argument.
In either case, then, it is not enough to know only *that X is* but that
additional reasons must be given for *why X is*. Nor can one deny that
this requirement, enshrined in the well-worn philosophical principle of
sufficient reason, is a commonplace of our experience; and that doctors,
to give but one example, while they are willing to admit that there are
diseases with unknown causes, are less likely to admit that there are
diseases without causes. But the operational success of this principle,
particularly evident in the empirical sciences, should not obscure us to the
fact that the requirement to find an explanation is *not a logical requirement*;
and that accordingly it is not a matter of *logical necessity* either that such
explanations will be found or, more importantly, that such explanations
exist to be found. We may conclude, in other words, that the principle
of sufficient reason is an assumption that many feel obliged to make
in order to avoid the conclusion that the world is pointless, and that
this assumption is both intellectually and emotionally satisfying; but to
conclude that the world is pointless is not in itself contradictory. When
therefore, Aquinas and Paley present us with the dilemma 'Either there
is a God or the universe is ultimately inexplicable', it is not an error of
logic to conclude that the universe is ultimately inexplicable and that
accordingly there is no God.

This, I hope, makes clear that the atheistic alternative, while
undoubtedly for many psychologically uncomfortable, is logically
legitimate and that it is therefore permissible to suppose that the world
may contain brute facts that cannot be explained or that the world itself
is ultimately inexplicable and that it may just happen to be. But which of
these alternatives is the more plausible? Is our world better explained by

saying that it is of divine origin, created and designed by an omnipotent God, or should we eliminate God altogether and say that we live in a world which provides explanation of itself, disclosed to us in the material and variable conditions of our immediate reality? Thus the theistic and atheistic explanations stand as contesting alternatives; but the question now to ask is: Which has the greater explanatory power?

As we saw in Chapter Two, by the seventeenth century the pendulum had already begun to swing away from the Aristotelian system of Creator and First Cause towards a mechanico-materialistic interpretation of the natural world. This shift – supported, we recall, by what Joseph Glanville (1636-1680) was to call the rediscovery of 'the more excellent Hypotheses of Democritus and Epicurus'[2] – did not at first manifest itself in any overt atheism: unsurprisingly, given the precedents of Bruno and Vanini; and when it did, the results could still be devastating for the author. Witness the case of the French philosopher, Julien Offray de la Mettrie (1707-1751). While his two most notorious books – *Histoire naturelle de l'âme* (1745) and *L'Homme machine* (1747) – fall short of explicit atheism, their distinctly anti-metaphysical tone, denunciation of the creator-God and uniform materialism led to persecution and exile, first in Holland and finally in Prussia under the protection of Frederick the Great. Some, indeed, were so fearful of reprisals that they were prepared to live a double life. Here the outstanding example is Jean Meslier (1664-1729), priest of Etrépigny in the Ardennes, and perhaps the most remarkable apostate of his age. Outraged by the hypocritical life he had been condemned to lead during his life, Meslier prepared three copies of a very lengthy *Mémoire* (better known as his *Testament*) to be published posthumously. In it he begs the forgiveness of his parishioners for confirming them in the 'lies' and 'deceptions' of Christianity and proceeds to a methodical refutation of miracles, the divinity of Jesus, the authority of the New Testament, revelation, the dogmas of the Church, Christian morality, the immortality of the soul, and much else besides. Throughout, the *Testament* is buttressed by the principles of atheistic materialism. The absurdity of the 'Unmoved Mover' and the fiction of separate mental and spiritual realms are replaced by the eternality and universality of matter constantly in motion; and all known phenomena are reduced to particular configurations of particles or to what Meslier calls 'the continual fermentation of being'. The scandal caused by Meslier's 'counter-confession' was rapidly covered up by the ecclesiastical authorities; but his ideas were widely circulated in the eighteenth century through the text published in 1762 by Voltaire (1694-1778) under the title *Extrait*

---

2   *Vanity of Dogmatizing* (1661), quoted by Basil Wiley, *The Seventeenth Century Background*, New York, Columbia University Press, 1934, p.7.

Jean Meslier

des sentiments de Jean Meslier. Despite being described by Voltaire as 'the most singular phenomenon ever seen among all the meteors fatal to the Christian religion', Meslier's extreme atheism was too much even for him. For though Voltaire's anti-Christian *Sermon des cinquante* ('Sermon of the Fifty', 1762) shares many of Meslier's targets – later to become even more pronounced in his *Dictionnaire philosophique* (1764) – Voltaire entirely repudiated Meslier's materialist outlook and was indeed an enthusiastic defender of various versions of both the causal and design arguments. Thus in his edition of 1762 the atheistic framework of Meslier's Testament is entirely dismantled to accommodate Voltaire's more sympathetic approach; and it was not until 1864 that a three-volumed unexpurgated text appeared in Amsterdam.[3]

Voltaire's *Dictionnaire philosophique* also contains a refutation of the work that is invariably cited as the first avowedly atheistic book to appear in Christian Europe: *Le Système de la nature* (1770), written anonymously by Paul Henri, Baron d'Holbach (1723-1789).[4] His nickname, *le premier maître d'hôtel de la philosophie*, was certainly apt. His enormous wealth funded one of the most important and hospitable salons in Paris, which was to run for over thirty years, from the 1750s onwards. This became a famous meeting place for many of d'Holbach's fellow-contributors to

---

3   *La Testament de Jean Meslier*, ed. Rudolf Charles, Amsterdam, La Librairie Etrangère. For a rather exuberant account of Meslier's importance, see the French philosopher Michel Onfray, 'Jean Meslier and "The Gentle Inclination of Nature"', *New Politics*, 10, No.4, Winter 2006. According to Onfray, Meslier is the first atheist in Western history, the first deconstructionist of Christianity, and the first philosopher to announce the death of God. See also Andrew R. Morehouse, *Voltaire and Jean Meslier*, New Haven, Yale University Press, 1936. A play has been written about Meslier by David Hall.

4   As the British equivalent, published in London twelve years later, David Berman names the *Answer to Dr Priestley's letters to a philosophical unbeliever*, generally attributed to the Liverpool physician, Matthew Turner. At any rate, the author is quite explicit in his debt to *The System of Nature*, then thought to be by Mirabeau. See *A History of Atheism in Britain: From Hobbes to Russell*, London and New York, Routledge, 1990, p.110.

the *Encyclopédie*, most notably
Denis Diderot, and for other
intellectuals invited from
abroad: Adam Smith, Horace
Walpole and Edward Gibbon,
to mention just a few, were all
wined and dined. Almost from
the first d'Holbach made no
attempt to hide his militant
materialist-atheism, attacking
Christianity and religion
generally in a series of books.
To avoid persecution almost
all were published abroad,
either anonymously or under
false names. These include
Christianity Unveiled (1761), *The*

Baron d'Holbach

Holy Disease (1768), and, in 1770, his most famous work, *The System of
Nature*. Such was the outcry on publication that the Catholic Church in
France threatened the Crown with the withdrawal of its financial support
unless circulation was suppressed, and the book was publicly burned.
Undaunted, d'Holbach provided a popular summary of his radical ideas
in his *Common Sense or Natural Ideas Opposed to Supernatural* (1772), and
in 1776 published his *Universal Morality*, in which he denounces any
suggestion that religion is a prerequisite of morality.

Nicknamed 'The Atheist's Bible', *The System*, while unoriginal in ideas,
is notorious for d'Holbach's thoroughgoing atheistic materialism and his
attempt to expose religion as a superstition foisted upon the weak and
gullible by deluded visionaries and fanatics. Here the atheistic tendencies
of the eighteenth century find their most blatant expression, with wide
circulation ensuring that, for the first time, an undisguised attack upon
religion as the source of all human evils was openly discussed without
fear of official reprisal. Seeing in the universe nothing save matter in
spontaneous movement, it ridicules any suggestion of a life after death
and offers a naturalistic account of the origins of religion strongly
reminiscent of the criticisms of classical times: that it issues from fear
and ignorance, fear of the unknown and ignorance of the laws of
causation. D'Holbach is therefore particularly scathing of any attempt to
see divine initiative as the necessary prerequisite of the order observed
in the natural world, and is accordingly totally dismissive of the watch-
universe analogy, which was to be deployed by Paley thirty-two years
later. D'Holbach's preference for atheistic naturalism over theism is, as

he explains, in part due to the economy of explanation apparent in the one but not in the other. For why adopt, as an explanation of *material* phenomena, an *immaterial* being, which is even more extraordinary than the things it is said to explain? A more parsimonious view is to conclude that the universe is all that there is, and that accordingly everything to be explained will be explicable in terms of what that universe contains.

> Nature is not a blind cause; she never acts by chance; nothing that she does would ever be considered fortuitous, by him who should understand her mode of action – who had a knowledge of her resources – who was intelligent in her ways. Every thing that she produces is strictly necessary – is never more than a consequence of her eternal, immutable laws; all is connected in her by invisible bonds; every effect we witness flows necessarily from its cause, whether we are in a condition to fathom it, or whether we are obliged to let it remain hidden from our view. It is very possible there should be ignorance on our part; but the words spirit, intelligence, will not remedy this ignorance; they will rather redouble it, by arresting our research; by preventing us from conquering those impediments which obstruct us in probing the natural causes of the effects, with which our visual faculties bring us acquainted.[5]

Here d'Holbach is doing no more than underscoring what had already been said to even greater effect by his contemporary, and the most philosophically distinguished of his dinner-guests, the Scot, David Hume (1711-1776).[6] Admittedly, within the atheistic tradition Hume occupies a problematic position. From one perspective he stands not as an atheist but as the supreme representative of eighteenth-century scepticism, and a scepticism, moreover, not of the extreme pyrrhonistic brand – which denied the very possibility of knowledge altogether and so relapsed into

---

5   *TAC*: 108-109

6   The famous story of Hume dining with d'Holbach is told by Denis Diderot (1713-1784), who was present: 'The first time that M. Hume found himself at the table of the Baron he was seated beside him. I do not know for what purpose the English (*sic*) philosopher took it into his head to remark to the Baron that he did not believe in atheists, that he had never seen any. The Baron said to him: 'Count how many we are here.' We are eighteen. The Baron added: 'It is not too bad a showing to be able to point out to you fifteen at once: the three others have not made up their minds.' Quoted by E. Mossner, *Life of David Hume*, Oxford, 1970. David Berman thinks that the story should not be taken at face value, and that, decoded, Hume's message 'amounted to a repudiation of the word "atheism" and an affirmation of something close to atheism'. (*Op.cit.*, p.103).

a quietist state of suspended judgment[7] – but of a more judicious kind, which does not say that no knowledge is possible but rather that what knowledge of the world is obtainable is restricted to the sum of our conscious experience, to our feelings and habits. This restriction, however, when viewed from another perspective, has a net result of enormous significance and explains why Hume holds his place within the atheistic canon. For the restriction of knowledge to our conscious experience means that, being now unable

David Hume

to obtain any experience of the nature of God or of the origin of the universe, no case for the 'religious hypothesis', or indeed for any metaphysical system, can be deployed with any cognitive certainty. On these grounds, Hume dismisses the arguments from cause and design. His objections first appear in his *A Treatise of Human Nature* (1739-1740), and then in his *Enquiry Concerning Human Understanding* (1748); but they receive their fullest expression in his *Dialogues Concerning Natural Religion* (1779), which on advice from Adam Smith was published posthumously. The criticisms that Hume now advances cannot be overestimated and for many philosophers they remain decisive. Space here forbids a lengthy account of them; but the following numbered progression of arguments will, I hope, be sufficient for our purposes.[8]

1   Both the causal and design arguments depend on the important presupposition that nature is uniform: 'that instances, of which we have had no experience, must resemble those, of which we have had experience, and that the course of nature continues always uniformly the same'.[9] But this general principle of uniformity, says Hume, cannot

---

7   See above, p.26

8   The text of the *Dialogues* is available at www.gutenberg.com and in the edition prepared by Norman Kemp Smith, London, Thomas Nelson, 1947. See also *TAC*: 114-120

9   *A Treatise of Human Nature* (1739), ed. L.A. Selby-Bigge, London, Oxford University Press, 1965, p.89.

be logically justified. For while the principle may, perfectly properly, lead us to assume that the future will resemble the past, and while it does undoubtedly play an important role in the organization of our everyday affairs, no 'necessary connection' in fact holds between them. It is rather that our constant experiencing of the same sequence of events – that whenever we meet with an A it has been followed by a B – creates in us a 'habit' or 'custom' of expecting that this will always be the case. And the same can be said of the relation between cause and effect. That every event must have a cause is taken for granted not because this causal principle is either intuitively obvious or demonstrable but because, here too, there is a 'determination of the mind' or psychological disposition in this instance to think in a causal way, which assumes that there must be an actual and necessary link between one event and another, whereas in fact none is either self-evident or demonstrable. Thus there is no inconsistency in holding that nature is not uniform, while any argument from experience that says that it is (Aquinas) is presupposing what it must first establish.

2 The claim that God is the single and ultimate cause of the universe is equally fallacious. 'But the WHOLE you say, wants a Cause. . . . Did I show you the particular causes of each individual in a collection of twenty particles of matter, I should think it very unreasonable, should you afterwards ask me, what was the cause of the whole twenty. That is sufficiently explained in explaining the cause of the parts'.[10] Logicians call this the 'fallacy of composition': it consists in claiming that, since every member of a class has a certain property, the class as a whole has the same property. Examples are: 'Every man has a mother; therefore the human race has a mother' or 'Every member of that football team is great; therefore that team is great'.[11] What is interesting about this fallacy is that, with different content, no fallacy is committed at all (e.g., 'Every member of the constituency voted Labour; therefore it is a Labour constituency'). Hume's point,

---

10 *Dialogues Concerning Natural Religion*, edited with an Introduction by Norman Kemp Smith, London, Thomas Nelson & Sons, 1947, pp.190-191.

11 The same mistake is committed in the 'quantifier-shift' fallacy. Here particular quantifiers (like 'some' or 'every') shift position during the course of the argument, moving from premise to conclusion. So: 1) *Every* member M of a group bears the relation R to *some* X; 2) Therefore, *some* particular X bears the relation R to *every* M. Or: 1) *Every* member of the class is loved by *some* one; 2) Therefore, there is *some* one who loves *every* one – doubtless the all-embracing Super-Lover! But, as with the fallacy of composition, if we reverse the components, no fallacy is committed: 1) There is *some* one who loves *every* one; 2) Therefore *every* one is loved by *some* one. These examples show how easy it is to commit the fallacy.

however, is that if, as in the causal argument, the explanation of the existence of each object in the universe is said to leave the existence of the universe unexplained, then the fallacy is committed. So, to give a well-known example, if five Eskimos are in New York, and we can explain why each Eskimo is there, no explanation is required to explain why the group as a whole is there.[12] Nor is it difficult to see why the fallacy is often committed. Collective words like 'group', 'class', 'world' or 'universe' often function in sentences as if they refer to specific objects; and it is therefore tempting to suppose that we can ask for a causal explanation of a group or class in the same way that we can ask for the causal explanation of a particular thing, like a tree or a house. But that is not the case, the reason being that the group is not something different from its membership; and that accordingly to explain the activity of the individual members is the same as to explain the activities of the group.

3 But even if this last point is not accepted, and we repeat that only an explanatory ultimate, lying outside the finite series of contingent things, can provide a sufficient reason for the existence of the universe, for why there should be therefore something and not nothing – for why, in other words, there should be any Eskimos at all to be in New York, or why indeed there should be a New York to have them there – Hume replies with a further objection, which again underlines his insistence that cosmological explanations should be anchored in experience. The demand for an explanatory ultimate to explain the universe as a whole is fulfilled with an identification of God as First Cause, but one in which the question, 'What, then, caused God?' is ruled out as inadmissible. In other words, God is presumed to be the only candidate for the job of First Cause. But why stop here? For if God can be self-caused, why cannot the universe itself be self-caused? This possibility, which has the great merit of assuming that nothing can exist apart from the totality of all existing things (i.e., the universe), requires no supernatural agent or divine author: the world, evolving from the primordial supply of matter, actualizes itself. And this alternative has the further merit of never extending itself beyond the realm of sense-experience within which it operates, of never assuming on the basis of our immediate experience of the operations of cause and effect that these operations can, as it were, overreach themselves and have equal application in a realm of which we have no direct experience but within which, it is said, exists the Uncaused

---

12 Given by Paul Edwards in his 'Introduction', *A Modern Introduction to Philosophy*, ed. Paul Edwards and Arthur Pap, New York, The Free Press, 1965, p.380.

Cause.[13] It is not therefore that God does not exist but rather that we have, within the limits imposed by Hume's scepticism, no means of assessing the validity of any argument that says that he exists.

4 Hume's criticisms of the design argument are similarly incisive. He first addresses the crucial analogy made between the universe and a machine, which is the initial step, we recall, towards the conclusion that both are the products of a purposive intelligence. But the analogy is unsound. First of all, the uniqueness of the universe weakens any claim that it resembles any artifact, be it a watch, house or a ship. For while we are able to judge from within our experience that watchmakers make watches and builders build houses, we have no experience of a plurality of universes from which we may infer that it is gods (or a God) that make universes. Nor indeed can we even assume that the feature of the universe which believers take to be evidence of a designer at work — namely, the order and regularities evident in nature — pertain in fact to the universe as a whole. 'A very small part of this great system, during a very short time, is very imperfectly discovered to us: and do we thence pronounce decisively concerning the origin of the whole?'[14]

5 But if we do wish to press the analogy, on the assumption that *like effects have like causes*, what are the grounds for concluding that the designer of the universe was an infinite, omnipotent, eternal and incorporeal being? Our experience is rather that machines are made by mortal, corporeal and human beings, either male or female, usually working together and invariably making mistakes, achieving the final product only through a process of gradual improvement. Why then should we not conclude that the world is similarly due to the combined efforts of many gods; that it is perhaps the 'first rude essay of some infant deity, who afterwards abandoned it' or 'the production of old age and dotage in some superannuated Deity', whose death left it to self-regulate. Why should not many worlds 'have been botched and bungled, throughout an eternity, ere this system was struck out?'[15]

6) All these criticisms are important; but it is Hume's next that, for the future development of positive atheism, has attained the greatest significance, foreshadowing the single most persistent and forceful objection to be levelled against the design argument from the nineteenth

---

13 A point elevated by Immanuel Kant (1724-1804) into a major epistemological doctrine: 'The principle of causality has no meaning and no criterion for its application save only in the sensible world. But in the cosmological proof it is precisely in order to enable us to advance beyond the sensible world that it is employed.' *Critique of Pure Reason* (1781), trans. Norman Kemp Smith, London, Macmillan, 1929, p.511.

14 *Dialogues,* p.149

15 *Ibid.,* pp.167

century until the present day. For Aquinas and Paley the ordering of means to ends in nature is inexplicable without a purposive Creator. Hume now demonstrates the fallibility of this connection by proposing other schemes, lying entirely within the fold of our experience, which would account for the order observed. Some of these, admittedly, are suggested very much with tongue in cheek, but one of them stands out; and this, significantly enough, re-introduces us to the by now familiar atomic theory of Epicurus, in which the universe evolves out of a primordial and immeasurable plurality of uncreated and indivisible particles. 'Thus the universe goes on for many ages in a continued succession of chaos and disorder. But is it not possible that it may settle at last . . . so as to preserve an uniformity of appearance, amidst the continual motion and fluctuation of its parts?'[16] This possibility weakens the analogy between world and artifact almost beyond recovery: the analogy can no longer be upheld if the effects can be accounted for by other means. Once again, therefore, we have to decide between two rival hypotheses: between, on the one hand, *authentic design* (i.e., the world is the product of a designer) and, on the other, *apparent design* (i.e., the world has the appearance of design but is in fact the product of chance). The evidence for each alternative remains the same – the fact of order – but this evidence is insufficient to support one hypothesis over the other.[17] This conclusion, it must be said, is not a recipe for outright atheism – Hume's scepticism prevents him from going quite that far – but then neither is it entirely open-ended. Indeed, the weighting thus far has been so entirely against the theistic use of analogy that we can with some certainty deduce – particularly when coupled with the relevant biographical evidence – that Hume's own private sympathies were entirely for an undesigned re-creative natural system of nature, in which the only ultimate is the universe itself; or rather, that no analogical argument can lead to the discovery of a new and qualitatively different reality; and certainly not to a supra-empirical reality utterly distinct from those ordinary empirical experiences from which the existence of the universe was first inferred.

---

16 *Ibid.*,p.184.

17 To suppose that it does is, indeed, to commit the fallacy of the 'affirmation of the consequent'. The logical form of this is: 'A implies B; B is true; therefore A is true.' Or: 'When Max has had no food, he gets angry; Max is angry; therefore Max has had no food'. The fallacy is fairly obvious, given that there may be a whole host of reasons, quite apart from indigestion, that account for Max's irritability. The fallacy operative in the design argument is the same: it too specifies a single cause for the given effect when in fact there may be more than one antecedent which leads to a particular consequent.

What, of course, is missing is that, at the time of Hume's proposal, no adequate scientific hypothesis existed to show how a natural system of nature could account for the intricacy and order of the world; and until a convincing body of evidence was forthcoming in support of this naturalist alternative, the religious explanation of intelligent design would continue to attract support. But all this was to change eighty-three years after Hume's death, with the publication in 1859 of the *Origin of Species* by Charles Darwin (1809-1882). Darwin's primary contribution to the demise of the design argument was to lend detailed scientific support to Hume's philosophical speculations about the diversity of causal explanation, and to provide a mechanism that could show that at least one of Hume's tentative explanations for the appearance of design – the so-called Epicurean hypothesis – far from being absurd, had in fact scientific support. This was provided by the theory of natural selection, an explanatory, self-regulating and entirely mechanical theory that could explain the evolution of species. The living organisms and intricate structures so admired by theologians did not emerge from the care taken by a divine being plotting the course of his creation, but evolved from a gradual process of species modification over enormous periods of time, of an 'adaptation to the environment' operating on whole populations of organisms, in which only those with beneficial modifications would survive in the competitive struggle for existence.

> If under changing conditions of life organic beings present individual differences in almost every part of their structure, and this cannot be disputed; if there be, owing to their geometrical rate of increase, a severe struggle for life at some age, season, or year, and this certainly cannot be disputed; then, considering the infinite complexity of the relations of all organic beings to each other and to their conditions of life, causing an infinite diversity in structure, constitution, and habits, to be advantageous to them, it would be an extraordinary fact if no variations had ever occurred useful to each being's own welfare, in the same manner as so many variations have occurred useful to man. But if variations useful to any organic being ever do occur, assuredly individuals thus characterized will have the best chance of being preserved in the struggle for life; and for the strong principle of inheritance, these will tend to produce offspring similarly characterised. This principle of preservation, or the survival of the fittest, I have called Natural Selection.[18]

---

18 *The Origin of Species by Means of Natural Selection*, 6th edition, London, John Murray, 1888, pp.102-103.

The scandal of Darwinism to the religious minds of the nineteenth century was not merely to be told that human beings derive from the same stock as animals, but to be informed additionally that the prime mover in the cosmic process was not purpose but chance, in which the survival of any particular species depended on the degree to which it could adapt to the particular environment in which it found itself. This conclusion fleshed out the atomistic theories first first presented in classical antiquity

Charles Darwin

and later used by Hume. Once again it is not *authentic* design that we see in the world around us but *apparent* design, in which chance and adjustment to circumstance determine the order that exists. This demolished the basis of purposive explanation. The sting of the theory, as Darwin himself makes clear, lies not so much then in the supposition that species develop gradually over vast stretches of time but in the suggestion that it is mechanical and haphazard factors that govern this development.

> Although I did not think much about the existence of a personal God until a considerably later period of my life, I will here give the vague conclusions to which I have been driven. The old argument from design in nature, as given in Paley, which formerly seemed to me so conclusive, fails, now that the law of natural selection has been discovered. We can no longer argue that, for instance, the beautiful hinge of a bivalve shell must have been made by an intelligent being, like the hinge of a door by man. There seems to be no more design in the variability of organic beings and in the action of natural selection, than in the course which the wind blows.[19]

Darwin's theory of natural selection has emerged from the nineteenth into the twentieth and twenty-first centuries as the single most widely

---

19 'Autobiography' (1903) in *Charles Darwin and T.H. Huxley: Autobiographies*, edited with an Introduction by Gavin de Beer, London, Oxford University Press, 1974, p.70.

canvassed argument deployed against the notion of a designing deity; beginning from biology the evolutionary hypothesis has evolved into a fully comprehensive and totally mechanistic interpretation of nature of unique explanatory power, corroborated in a great variety of disciplines: for example, in molecular biology and genetics, which has revealed the mechanism of inheritance in the nucleic acid called DNA; or in the geological documentation of a common ancestry in the fossil record, which has provided direct evidence of evolutionary transitions – of, for example, the evolution of terrestrial amphibians from fishes or of mammals from reptiles. But set within the even grander and more all-encompassing perspective of 'cosmic evolution', biological evolution is now seen as an important but yet minor part of an evolutionary scheme of truly universal dimensions in the arrangement of the solar system and galaxies, in which the cosmos – 'all that is or ever was or ever will be', to quote Carl Sagan[20] – remains subject to the determinants of time, chance and natural law, and so without design or a predictable destiny.

This is admittedly a long way from Darwin's original hypothesis. All that needs to be said, however, is that in all these neo-evolutionary applications preference is rarely given to a divine explanation for either terrestrial or astronomical phenomena. Small wonder, then, that the overwhelming majority of scientists has dismissed any attempt to resuscitate the theistic option of a creator God and that they have become increasingly vocal in their attack upon the more recent theories of 'intelligent design', as exemplified by Michael Behe's 'irreducible complexity' and William Dembski's 'design inference'.[21] Among these critics special mention should be made of Stephen Jay Gould, Peter Atkins, Louis Wolpert, Victor Stenger, Daniel Dennett, and, most militant of all, Richard Dawkins.

Before leaving the design argument I should like to refer briefly to one modern variant, which has received wide currency. This is the so-called 'fine-tuning' argument, sometimes also known as the *anthropic teleological argument*. Here the infinite range of conditions that would make life impossible is contrasted with the extraordinary improbability of achieving those conditions to make life actual. The Oxford mathematician Roger Penrose has estimated, for instance, that the probability of a universe with our particular set of physical properties is one part in one followed by 10^{123} decimal places.[22] The fine-tuning argument therefore rejects the

20 *Cosmos*, New York, Random House, 1980, p.4.

21 See Behe, *Darwin's Black Box: The Biochemical Challenge to Evolution*, New York, Free Press, 1996; and Dembski, *The Design Inference*, Cambridge, Cambridge University Press, 1998,

22 *The Emperor's New Mind*, Oxford, Oxford University Press, 1989, p.343.

theory of coincidence on grounds of the extreme unlikelihood of our world and human beings (*anthropoi*) appearing from random evolution. A much more plausible explanation is to invoke the agency of a divine being, who has fine-tuned or custom-made the laws and constants of nature for the creation of intelligent life.

As I have indicated elsewhere,[23] I regard this argument as very weak. Three criticisms are worth highlighting. First, a counter-argument to the anthropic calculation can be mounted to show that the extreme statistical improbability of any number of mundane events does not preclude their origin by chance. John Allen Paulos estimates that the probability of receiving a particular bridge hand of thirteen cards is approximately one in six-hundred billion – a statistical enormity that provides no reason to believe that behind the appearance of random dealing lies some bodiless super-dealer.[24] Second, in order to support the view that this fine-tuned universe is best explained by the operation of an intelligent agent, we should need some past experience of the genesis of other worlds from which to draw this inference. But to adapt Hume's previous objection, we have no such experience, and the only place where we have thus far observed the constants to be right is in only one world in one universe, which is ours. If we assume, however, that there may well exist outside our observational scope an infinite number of other universes, or other regions of space-time, each varying in their initial conditions and fundamental constants, it becomes less surprising that one of them is life-permitting, and that this particular 'fine-tuned' universe may, for all we know, be one microscopic part of an infinite and completely random whole. But quite why we should assume that this (largely unknown) macrocosm should mirror the (largely known) microcosm is hard to see.

My third criticism is this. While the 'fine-tuning' argument leads in one direction – that intelligent life without a creator is highly improbable – we may here invoke an 'incompetent tuning' argument, which leads in another: that the often adverse conditions of life and the innumerable instances of organic malfunctions – e.g., the existence of genetic disorders such as Huntington's Chorea and the inability of DNA to self-repair – lead us to suppose that the responsible deity is inefficient, malevolent and unworthy of worship. For Darwin it was the paradigm-example of the *Ichneumonae* that convinced him of God's profligate injustice. This is a parasitic insect group whose females lay their eggs in or on the larvae or pupae of other insects, often moths and butterflies, whose young then proceed to feed on the fats and body fluids of their hosts, literally eating them alive. Paley, I should add, believed that he could resolve this

---

23 *QG*, p.135
24 *Innumeracy: Mathematical Illiteracy and Its Consequences*, 1989.

kind of difficulty. For, after all, the fact that the watch can and does
sometimes go wrong does not invalidate the claim that it is designed.
So much, of course, is true. But it clearly does make a difference to our
understanding of the watchmaker if what goes wrong is not seen to
be merely excessive but *the primary mechanism by which the watch operates.*
This is where the evolutionary explanation conclusively out-distances
the theistic explanation. According to Darwin, the mechanism by which
species evolve is the process of natural selection, and this process is
frequently wasteful and invariably cruel. So long as this is assumed, we
must then suppose that the God implied by evolution, far from being
benevolent, is almost totally unconcerned for the welfare of his creatures
and almost totally unmoved by the suffering which he has planned for
them.

4
The Problem of Evil

i. Introduction

The existence of evil in the world is regarded by most atheists as the principal objection to the existence of God, called by the Roman Catholic theologian Hans Küng the 'rock of atheism'. By 'evil' is meant the fact of pain and suffering and the 'problem' that it poses for religious belief is not hard to see. How can evil exist in a world created by an omnipotent and omni-benevolent God? For the positive atheist this question exposes an insuperable inconsistency within religious belief, thereby invalidating the claim that any God exists. Nor, I should add, is discussion confined to the philosophical literature: the Old Testament deals with it in the Old Testament book of *Job*, as do numerous works of fiction, three of which should be mentioned in particular: Primo Levi's *If this is a Man* (1947) Albert Camus' *The Plague* (1948) and Fydor Dostoevsky's *The Brothers Karamazov* (1880), the last-named providing perhaps the most famous and haunting exposition of the problem ever written.[1]

To clarify the issue at hand, evil is further and traditionally subdivided into two types: 1) there is *natural* or *non-moral* evil; and 2) there is *moral evil*. Non-moral evil refers to suffering due to natural calamities, that is, to events outside man's control, i.e., through earthquakes, hurricanes, floods, disease etc. A classic example of such phenomena is the Tsunami of 2004, which killed approximately 225,000 people in eleven countries. Historically, however, the most significant of such events was the Lisbon earthquake of 1755, in which perished or were injured 90,000 people out of a total population of 230,000. The fact that this happened in a Catholic country, on the day of a Catholic festival, and that it destroyed all the churches in the capital gave to the event a particular theological and philosophical resonance, with far-reaching cultural implications. For Voltaire it was sufficient to cure him for ever of any lingering optimism that this was, after all, 'the best of all possible worlds'; a suggestion he attacks in his *Poème sur le Désastre de Lisbonne* (1756) and ridicules in his play *Candide* (1759).

---

1 See *TAC*: 152-161.

But we have come across natural evil before, although admittedly not on such an immediate and dramatic scale. Darwin's theory of natural selection charts a process of unparalleled brutality, haphazard in operation, and subject only to the vagaries of environment; and his analysis of the evolution of new species under such adverse conditions was sufficient to undermine Darwin's religious beliefs. William Paley, we recall, thought he could resolve the difficulty: the calamities that occur within the natural world may be construed as instances of the watch going wrong. But this is to miss Darwin's point: these cruelties are part and parcel of the mechanism of the watch. *This is how the watch works* – as he makes clear in a letter to Asa Gray:

> An innocent and good man stands under a tree and is killed by a flash of lightning. Do you believe (and I should really like to hear) that God *designedly* killed this man? Many and most persons do believe this; I can't and don't. If you believe so, do you believe that when a swallow snaps up a gnat that God designed that that particular swallow should snap up that particular gnat at that particular instant? I believe that the man and the gnat are in the same predicament. If the death of neither man nor gnat are designed, I see no reason to believe that their *first* birth or production should be necessarily designed.[2]

Natural evil lies outside human control but moral evil is the direct result of it. Here the suffering produced is a consequence of individual or collective action, i.e., killing, war, mental and physical torture etc. The classic example of this type of evil is the Nazi programme during the Second World War, known as the 'Holocaust', in which six-million Jews perished – an act of such incomparable brutality that it has tended to obscure other examples of genocidal suffering: in Turkey (1915-1918: 1,500,000 Armenian deaths); in Bosnia-Herzegovina (1992-1995: 200,000 Muslim deaths); in Rwanda (1994: 500,000 Tutsi deaths) and more recently in the Dafur region of Western Sudan (from 2003: 450,000 deaths). To these events we must add those in which the distinction between moral and non-moral evil is less clear-cut, in which human and non-human acts conspire to produce the resulting catastrophe. An example of this is cyclone Nargis that hit Burma in May 2008. Estimates put the number of dead or missing at over 140,000: a figure undoubtedly increased by the reluctance of the ruling military junta to call in emergency aid.

Any theistic attempt to resolve the alleged incompatibility between the existence of God and the existence of evil is called, following

---

2   *The Life and Letters of Charles Darwin*, ed. Francis Darwin, John Murray, 1903, Vol. 1, p.315.

Leibniz, a *theodicy* (from the Greek, *theos* [God] + *dike* [justice] and down the centuries many classic theodicies have been offered. Some of these may be discarded from the outset. The first two I should like to mention resolve the problem of evil by evading it altogether, that is, by the simple expedient of denying one of its components: that no evil exists or that no omnipotent God exists. The first alternative is found, for example, in the teachings of Christian Science. The founder of the movement, Mary

Mary Baker Eddy

Baker Eddy (1821-1910) maintained that disease was unreal and the product of ignorance. 'Evil is but an illusion, and it has no real basis. Evil is a false belief, God is not its author'.[3] Since, however, the belief that suffering was an illusion carried with it the further belief that disease was unreal, this teaching was medically hazardous and had disastrous consequences for many of its adherents: unsurprisingly membership of the sect has declined rapidly. Nor, indeed, does the claim that evil is an illusion resolve anything. For if evil is the product of ignorance and illusion, then such ignorance and illusion remain the evils incompatible with God's omniscient goodness. The second alternative, admittedly, has more mileage. This is the Manichaean heresy of di-theism, which appeared in Persia in the second century and which takes its name from its founder Mani (c. A.D. 215-176). This asserts that evil is the product of a struggle between two non-omnipotent powers, the one good and the other evil, neither of which can overcome the other. It was, however, Augustine of Hippo (354-430) who, despite his own initial membership of the sect, denounced the belief as a 'shocking and detestable profanity', one which must necessarily impugn the rule of God as the universal and sole sovereign of creation. While modern theologians have almost totally rejected the claims of a supernatural evil being (Satan) as the source of evil, it is worth noting that recent so-called 'process' theologians, most notably Charles Hartshorne (1897-2000), have resolved the dilemma along not entirely dissimilar lines, admittedly rejecting any personification of evil but also denying traditional concepts of divine omnipotence.[4]

---

3 *Science and Health with Key to the Scriptures*, Boston, Mass., 1875, p.480.

4 See Hartshorne, *Omnipotence and other Theological Mistakes*, Albany, State University of New York Press, 1984.

Two further theodicies deserve special mention. The first is the *punishment theodicy*, by which God allows or brings about evil as a punishment for wrongdoing. Closely allied to the biblical account of original sin, and mythologically expressed in the *Genesis* account of the expulsion of Adam and Eve from the Garden of Eden, this argument, as an article of faith, provides no satisfactory explanation of the original motive to sin and has unacceptable moral implications by making the distribution of suffering disproportionate, visiting the sins of the guilty parents upon their innocent children and thereby undermining the notion of a just God. By advocating retribution for sins committed, the theory is indiscriminate in its application, meting out punishment to those who have committed no crime or are incapable of doing so – e.g., those too young or too mentally deficient to take any moral responsibility for their actions – and in so doing employs a system of justice that our own courts would find repugnant.

The second theodicy has been mentioned briefly already. This is the 'best of all worlds' theodicy, associated with the philosopher and mathematician Gottfried Leibniz (1648-1716). Like Augustine before him, Leibniz begins with the claim that the world is the creation of an omnipotent and perfectly good God. This is developed into the parallel assertion that, being good, God would be contrary to his own nature if he did not create the best world possible. Or: the mind of God, like some vast calculating machine, is alone capable of surveying the infinite variety of possible worlds and, being good, has necessarily selected the best, that is, a world admittedly containing evil, but only that amount which is indispensable for the creation of the best possible world. Leibniz' reasoning here is that a world with evil may be better than one without evil, and that, just as in mathematics, 'an imperfection in a part may be necessary for a greater perfection in the whole'. As to the question of God's culpability for moral evil – namely, that God could have prevented suffering but does not – Leibniz introduces the notions of antecedent and consequent will. The former will is the divine will for good – e.g., that men should not sin – and the latter God's permitting will – e.g. that men should be allowed to sin for 'superior reasons'. Leibniz' point is that the creation of the best possible world can only be achieved within the context of the imperfections of his creatures. Thus the best plan of the universe must embrace certain evils, these 'disorders in the parts', that enhance the 'beauty of the whole'.

This argument, already ridiculed by Voltaire, is philosophically demolished by David Hume in his *Dialogues Concerning Natural Religion* (1779), to which we have already referred. Leibniz' argument is that what evil there is in the world must be both necessary and unavoidable. But this argument fails if it can be shown that not all evil is either essential or necessary. And this Hume proceeds to do in a section entitled 'The Four Circumstances of Evil'.[5] 1) We are told that pain acts as a warning-device, making all creatures 'vigilant in the great work of self-preservation'. But the same could just as easily have been achieved by a 'diminution of pleasure', prompting men and animals alike 'to seek that object, which is necessary to their subsistence'; 2) Pain is also assumed to be an unavoidable by-product of natural laws

Gottfried Leibniz

that overall produce beneficial results; but here too the slightest intervention by a benign deity would have created an immeasurably happier world, one in which, for example, ships would always reach their destinations, or good rulers would always enjoy sound health and a long life. 'A few such events as these, regularly and wisely conducted, would change the face of the world'. 3) A similar adjustment could be made in the powers and faculties of all animals, including men and women. The human species, for instance, although in bodily advantages the most deficient, is distinguished by a capacity to reason; why not, then, additionally increase our powers of concentration, capacity for work, levels of intellectual ability or talents for friendship? Again, the benefits from such slight modifications would be incalculable. 'But it is hard; I dare to repeat it, it is hard, that being placed in a world so full of wants and necessities; where almost every being and element is either our foe or refuses to give us their assistance; we should also have our own temper to struggle with, and should be deprived of that faculty which can alone fence against these multiplied evils'. 4) Finally, and most decisively, Hume points to those evils that arise from 'the inaccurate workmanship of all the springs and principles of the great machine of nature'. Here it is all a question of degree. For while it may be accepted that such things as wind, rain and heat are necessary for the maintenance of life, why is it that all these things, by excess or defect, can become so quickly the cause of ruin and misery: the wind the hurricane, the rain the flood, the heat the drought?

---

5 *Op.cit.*, pp. 204-211.

Hume's detailed catalogue of suffering makes Leibniz' solution to the problem of evil quite unacceptable as an explanatory hypothesis. For in each of the examples given by Hume the slightest alteration would greatly decrease the quantity of evil without affecting the desired quantity of good. And these examples place the theist in a difficult position: he or she must now show a justifying purpose for such suffering, and explain why suffering, Hume's examples notwithstanding, remains an indispensable component of the divine creation, and why an omnipotent and benevolent God did not choose other means of bringing about the same results. For Hume himself, if the goodness of God cannot be established *a priori*, then it must be established *a posteriori*, that is, on the basis of the empirical evidence before us; and here the evidence points away from any theistic explanation but rather to Hume's own preferred choice: of human beings at the mercy of an atomistic, epicurean world indifferent to whatever good or evil may exist within it.

> Look round the universe. What an immense profusion of beings, animated and organized, sensible and active! You admire this prodigious variety and fecundity. But inspect a little more narrowly these living existences, the only beings worth regarding. How hostile and destructive to each other! How insufficient all of them for their own happiness! How contemptible or odious to the spectator! The whole presents nothing but the idea of a blind nature, impregnated by a great vivifying principle, and pouring forth from her lap, without discernment or parental care, her maimed and abortive children.[6]

With these failed theodicies behind us, let us now return to the main debate. Modern commentators usually distinguish between two versions of the problem of evil: 1) the *logical form*: that the existence of evil is logically incompatible with God's existence; and 2) the *evidential form*: that, while not logically incompatible with the existence of God, the sheer weight and variety of suffering in the world make religious belief untenable.

ii. The Logical (or Deductive) Argument from Evil

This argument claims that there is a logical incompatibility between the existence of suffering and the existence of a being who in the Judaeo-Christian tradition is defined as possessing certain attributes, namely, omnipotence and omni-benevolence. The argument runs as follows: 1) If God, who is a benevolent and omnipotent being, exists, there would

---

6   *Ibid.*, p.211.

be no evil; 2) Evil exists; therefore 3) God does not exist. Lucretius, in his *De Rerum Natura*, cites Epicurus as the first exponent of a deductive argument from evil – hence this objection is sometimes called the 'Epicurean paradox' – but it is to Hume again that we must look for the most famous exposition. So in the *Dialogues* he writes: 'Epicurus' old questions are yet unanswered. Is he [God] willing to prevent evil, but not able? then he is impotent. Is he able, but not willing? then he is malevolent. Is he both able and willing? whence then is evil?'[7] Any confidence that Hume

J.L. Mackie

may have had that the logical problem would remain unresolved was, however, premature. This is because the leading modern exponent, the Australian atheist J.L. Mackie (1917-1981) acknowledged that this objection had been successfully refuted by an American, the Christian philosopher, Alvin Plantinga (b.1932). So important is this debate that some brief account must now be given of it.

Mackie presents his argument in an essay 'Evil and Omnipotence', which appeared in the journal *Mind* in 1955.[8] According to Mackie, the simplest form of the problem of evil – that God is omnipotent and wholly good, yet evil exists – does not bring out the full force of the contradiction. Mackie therefore introduces two further principles or 'quasi-logical rules' to show more precisely where the contradiction lies. His argument runs as follows: the problem of evil can only be resolved if at least one of these five propositions is jettisoned.

1 God is omnipotent: i.e., there are no limits to what an omnipotent being can do
2 God is wholly good: i.e., a wholly good being is opposed to evil in such a way that it eliminates evil as far as it can.
3 God is omniscient: i.e., if evil exists or is about to come into existence, then an omniscient being knows that it exists or is about to come into existence.
4 Evil exists.
5 God exists.

---

7 *Ibid.*, p.198.
8 Vol.64, pp. 200-212. The essay is reprinted in *The Problem of Evil*, ed. Marilyn McCord Adams and Robert Merrihew Adams, Oxford, Oxford University Press, 1990, pp.25-37.

When this occurs, however, the proposed solution is 'definitely fallacious'. Mackie reviews four such alternatives: that 1) 'Good cannot exist without evil' or 'Evil is necessary as a counterpart to good'; 2) 'Evil is necessary as a means to good'; 3) 'The universe is better with some evil in it than it could be if there were no evil'; and 4) 'Evil is due to human freewill'. It is the last of these to which Mackie devotes most attention; and rightly so because this introduces us to the first of the two great theodicies with which believers have traditionally defended their position. This is commonly called the *Free Will Defence*, according to which evil derives from the God-given ability of human beings to choose between good and evil acts.

Classically stated by Augustine of Hippo, in its usual formulation the Free Will Defence purports to be an explanation of moral and not non-moral evil – for many the Achilles heel of the argument, to which we shall return. The claim is that, despite the possibility of misuse, God gave humans the ability to make choices because a world with free choices is more desirable than one without them. It is this argument that Mackie challenges on the grounds that God could have created human beings with free will but *who were yet incapable of doing wrong*.

> I should ask this: if God has made men such that in their free choices they sometimes prefer what is good and sometimes what is evil, why could he not have made men such that they always freely choose the good? If there is no logical impossibility in a man's freely choosing the good on one, or on several, occasions, there cannot be a logical impossibility in his freely choosing the good on every occasion. God was not, then, faced with a choice between making innocent automata and making beings who, in acting freely, would sometimes go wrong: there was open to him the obviously better possibility of making beings who would act freely but always go right. Clearly, his failure to avail himself of this possibility is inconsistent with his being both omnipotent and wholly good.[9]

The objection to this hypothesis, which Mackie has in part anticipated, is that there is a contradiction in saying, on the one hand, that God has made us so that we must always act in a certain way, and, on the other, that we are also genuinely free and morally autonomous individuals. One cannot be both a mindless puppet and a free decision-making agent at the same time. But to this criticism Mackie has a reply. If it is being suggested that the moral freedom given by God to individuals is 'really free', then this must mean that God cannot control them and that

---

9   *Ibid.*, p.33.

therefore God is not omnipotent. What we have here, in other words, is an example of what Mackie calls the 'Paradox of Omnipotence': Can an omnipotent being make things which he cannot subsequently control? The most frequently quoted illustration of the paradox is the Paradox of the Stone: 'Can God create a rock so heavy that he cannot lift it?' This question, it would appear, cannot be answered in a way that is consistent with God's omnipotence. For if we say that God can create a rock so heavy that he cannot lift it, then it must be conceded that God lacks the power to lift that rock; and if we deny that God can create a rock so heavy that he cannot lift it, then it must be conceded that God lacks the power to create that rock. Either way there is something that God cannot do.[10]

Mackie's article of 1955 provided a core argument for philosophical atheists for the next twenty years – until, that is, 1974, in which year Alvin Plantinga published his *The Nature of Necessity* and his more accessible *God, Freedom, and Evil.* As Plantinga makes clear from the beginning, he is not, strictly speaking, engaged in a theodicy – a theodicy, to repeat, being an explanation for the presence of evil in a universe created by an omnipotent and perfectly good being – but in a *defence* against an alleged incompatibility between two propositions: these being 1) that an omnipotent and perfectly good being exists and 2) that evil exists. The consensus view is that in this Plantinga has succeeded, a philosophical defeat accepted by Mackie.

Mackie has argued that God did not take the logically possible option of creating human beings who always freely choose to do good. Plantinga replies that here Mackie is wrong to suppose that, since there is a *logically possible* world where free creatures always do good, God can *actualize* such a world. This is an example of what Plantinga calls 'Leibniz' lapse': that God must necessarily be able to actualize *all* possible worlds. But this is not the case. For although omnipotent, God cannot do the

---

10 Following an important article by James Rachels, an interesting addition can be made to Mackie's argument. A contradiction is said to arise from the conception of God as a being 'worthy of worship.' Since only a being with an 'unqualified claim to our obedience' is worthy of worship, the believer must be required to abdicate his autonomy or independent judgment. But since autonomy is an essential requirement of moral decision, no being who is worthy of worship can make this demand. Hence the contradiction within the ascribed property: either being a moral agent means that one cannot be a worshipper (i.e., subservient to God's commands) or being a worshipper means that one cannot be a moral agent. See Rachels, 'God and Human Attitudes', *Religious Studies*, 7, 1971, pp.325-337. Reprinted in *Divine Commands and Morality*, ed. Paul Helm, Oxford, Oxford University Press, 1981, pp.34-48.

logically impossible – for example, make 2+2=5 or squares round – and significantly to allow free will while yet eliminating suffering is also to do what is *logically impossible*. Plantinga's reasoning is as follows. For God to create a world in which human beings always choose the good would be incompatible with freedom, i.e., God would be *causing* them to do it and would thus be imposing a limit on what was possible. If God causes X to do Y, then X is not free with respect to Y because he cannot choose not to do Y. Thus it is logically impossible for people freely to do what they are caused by God to do. Plantinga later extends this argument by introducing the notion of 'transworld depravity'. This involves the claim that in any possible world where a person is free, that person would, at some time or other, act wrongly. Since, however, it is further logically possible that everybody may suffer from transworld depravity, then it is logically possible that God cannot create free beings who always do what is morally right. These arguments, Plantinga claims, expose the weakness of Mackie's criticism. While it is logically possible for God to create a state of affairs in which free agents always choose the good, it is not logically possible to ensure that the good always comes about since that would be logically inconsistent with the freedom of the agents. Therefore the existence of at least some evil is logically consistent with the existence of God.

> A world containing creatures who are sometimes significantly free (and freely perform more good than evil actions) is more valuable, all else being equal, than a world containing no free creatures at all. Now God can create free creatures, but he cannot cause or determine them to do only what is right. For if he does so, then they are not significantly free after all; they do not do what is right freely. To create creatures capable of moral good, therefore, he must create creatures capable of moral evil; and he cannot leave these creatures free to perform evil and at the same time prevent them from doing so. . . . The fact that these free creatures sometimes go wrong, however, counts neither against God's omnipotence nor against his goodness; for he could have forestalled the occurrence of moral evil only by excising the possibility of moral good.[11]

Mackie, in his *The Miracle of Theism* (1982) concedes that Plantinga has shown how God and evil can co-exist – that he has successfully resolved a logical problem – but that the substantive issue still remains unanswered. After all, as Plantinga himself has made clear, a defence is not a theodicy, and the reason why evil exists at all still remains to be explained. God

---

11 *The Nature of Necessity*, Oxford, Oxford University Press, 1974, pp.166-167.

may not be the author of evil and
cannot therefore be accused of
'malice aforethought'; but he is
still open to the charge of 'gross
negligence or recklessness' in not
foreseeing the consequences of
creating free individuals. There
thus remains what Mackie calls
the problem of 'unabsorbed
evils'.[12] We may list some. Undoubtedly there are many evils
– those in the moral category –
which are due to human actions;

Alvin Platinga

and the Free Will Defence may indeed go some way towards explaining
why such things as cheating, lying, torturing and murdering occur in
God's creation. If people are autonomous moral agents, then it does
seem plausible to claim that the gift of freedom enables people to commit
such immoral acts. But it is difficult see how this defence can explain evils
in the non-moral category, of why God should allow so many human
beings to be cheated of the benefits of life through no fault of their
own and succumb to congenital defects, paralysis, insanity and the like.
In what way will my moral autonomy be compromised if God tomorrow
completely eliminated cancer? Of course, it could be argued that this is
precisely what God is doing, as some kind of supervising editor of cancer
research; but this is of little comfort to those already dead or dying.
Plantinga's own response at this point is hardly satisfactory: it is possible,
he says, that such natural evils are produced by fallen angels, by Satan and
his demonic cohorts; a suggestion that would convert natural evil into a
form of moral evil. Well, certainly this remains a logical possibility. But
the claim that non-moral evil is in fact moral evil perpetrated by non-
human agents is very hard to take, and bears not only an unfortunate
resemblance to an earlier argument in which Satan made an appearance,
already discredited for impugning God's sovereignty, but carries with it
an unfortunate implication for Plantinga's own argument. Plantinga has
told us that evil is an unavoidable result of free actions: it is, as it were,
the price of freedom, which is the greater good. Orthodoxy similarly
ascribes the Fall of Satan to Satan's own autonomous action, but now
made irredeemably evil and incapable of ever producing good. Given
this scenario it is difficult to see why God should allow this demonic
figure to wreak such havoc while permanently denying to him alone the
chance of ever redeeming himself, of ever exercising his choice for good

12 *Op.cit.*, p.176

which, we are assured, is a necessary element of autonomy. This is, it seems to me, no more than an inversion of Mackie's original hypothesis: that God has here created a being who acts freely but always goes wrong.

iii. The Evidential (or Inductive) Argument from Evil.

Whether or not we accept that Plantinga has provided a successful reply to Mackie, most philosophers now hold that the logical argument from evil is redundant. Accordingly a major feature of recent literature is the shift away from this argument and towards an evidential counterpart. This evidential argument proceeds on a different tack and presents an inductive or probabilistic argument for the non-existence of God: that the existence of evil provides *prima facie* reasons for the probability, if not the possibility, that no God exists. The major contemporary exponent of this objection is the American philosopher, William Rowe (b.1931), whose argument proceeds as follows:

1 There exist instances of intense suffering which an omnipotent, omniscient being could have prevented without thereby preventing the occurrence of any greater good.
2 An omniscient, wholly good being would prevent the occurrence of any intense suffering it could, unless it could not do so without thereby preventing the occurrence of some greater good.

Therefore,

3 There does not exist an omnipotent, omniscient, wholly good being.[13]

The question now is not whether the existence of God and the existence of evil are logically incompatible but whether particular instances of excessive and pointless suffering renders the existence of God less likely. Rowe has made famous the example of a fawn slowly burning to death in a forest fire, and he admits that it is possible that an omnipotent and benevolent God could have a reason for allowing such a terrible thing to happen. He also accepts that there may be cases of moral and spiritual development impossible without suffering, except of course that this is not the case with the fawn. For here we are dealing with a particular example of suffering which does not result in any greater compensating good, i.e., a case that is not the consequence of human choice, is excessive to a degree, produces no beneficial effects, and which a good and omnipotent being could have prevented, had he so wished. Rowe concludes that the failure to find a morally justifiable reason for such gratuitous suffering is sufficient evidence that there is no reason, and that accordingly it is unlikely that God exists.

---

13 *The Philosophy of Religion*, Belmont, California, Wadsworth, 1978, pp.86-94.

In emphasizing the evidential basis of atheism – that the variety and profusion of evil in our world provides rational support for unbelief – Rowe is returning us to the historical mainstream of the debate, according to which God's non-existence can be assumed on the basis of certain empirical evidence. According to the atheistic authors thus far reviewed – from Lucretius down to Hume – the fact of gratuitous suffering, while it can be accommodated within the boundaries of an implacable and indifferent universe, cannot so easily sit within a world of divine

Percy Bysshe Shelley

origin. The presence of evil testifies to the absence of God; or, if not to his absence, then to his presence as an incompetent villain of sadistic temper. Those who subscribed to such views, however, trod warily, given the likely repercussions for those concerned; and it comes as no surprise to discover, as we have seen already, that d'Holbach's *System of Nature* (1770) should be published anonymously or that on advice Hume's *Dialogues* of 1779 should appear posthumously. Another important example is of the poet Percy Bysshe Shelley (1792-1822), perhaps the most famous of all British atheists. Brought up in a conventional Anglican household, Shelley was sent down from Oxford in 1811 for publishing his pamphlet 'The Necessity of Atheism', later expanded into his more philosophically refined *A Refutation of Deism*, circulated privately in 1814. Here Shelley attacks the moral bankruptcy of Christianity, and in doing so provides an interesting twist to the evidential argument against God, namely, that his omniscience never extended to foreseeing what barbarities Christianity would perpetrate upon mankind.

> I will admit that one prediction of Jesus Christ has been indisputably fulfilled. *I come not to bring peace upon earth, but a sword.* Christianity indeed has equalled Judaism in the atrocities, and exceeded it in the extent of its desolation. Eleven millions of men, women, and children, have been killed in battle, butchered in their sleep, burned to death at public festivals of sacrifice, poisoned, tortured, assassinated, and pillaged in the spirit of the Religion of Peace, and for the glory of the most merciful God.

In vain will you tell me that these terrible effects flow not from Christianity, but from the abuse of it. No such excuse will avail to palliate the enormities of a religion pretended to be divine. A limited intelligence is only so far responsible for the effects of its agency as it foresaw, or might have foreseen them; but Omniscience is manifestly chargeable with all the consequences of its conduct. Christianity itself declares that the worth of the tree is to be determined by the quality of its fruit. The extermination of infidels; the mutual persecutions of hostile sects; the midnight massacres and slow burnings of thousands, because their creed contained either more or less than the orthodox standard, of which Christianity has been the immediate occasion; and the invariable opposition which philosophy has ever encountered from the spirit of revealed religion, plainly show that a very slight portion of sagacity was sufficient to have estimated at its true value the advantages of that belief to which some Theists are unaccountably attached.[14]

Shelley is the most high-profile atheist of the early nineteenth century; but as the century advanced such views became more commonplace and more overt, largely as a result of the increasing Victorian conviction that all beliefs were fallible. This conviction carried with it the further demand only to assent to those propositions for which there was sufficient evidence. With the increasing professionalization of the scientific community, this demand became more insistent, and research proceeded into areas previously protected by religious authority, tradition and dogma. Darwin's investigations into the origin of species may have been the most prominent, but other researches, such as the geological exploration into the age of the Earth or the development of the theory of conservation of energy, only served to foster doubt on the literal inerrancy of scripture. The lawyer Sir James Fitzjames Stephen (1829-1894) argued that to assume that tradition, devoid of any evidential support, had any authority in religious matters was like 'keeping a corpse above ground because it was the dearest and most beloved of all objects when alive'.[15] Other leading intellectuals of the period, such as Sir James' brother, the agnostic Sir Leslie Stephen (1832-1904) or the politician Sir John Morley (1838-1923) or the first atheist Member of Parliament Charles Bradlaugh (1833-1891) may have expressed themselves less picturesquely; but all were positively evangelical in their adherence to the evidentialist principle,

---

14 Quoted in *Varieties of Unbelief*, ed. J.C.A. Gaskin, New York, Macmillan, 1989, p.119.

15 Cited in Leslie Stephen, *The Life of Sir James Fitzjames Stephen*, London, Smith, Elder, 1894, p.370

classically defined by perhaps the most strident of their group, the mathematician W.K. Clifford (1845-1879): 'it is wrong always, everywhere, and for anyone, to believe anything upon insufficient evidence'.[16] And in all these cases the existence of suffering, to which Victorian reforming and philanthropic sensibilities were particularly alert, provided the core evidence. If not alone sufficient to demonstrate the non-existence of God, it was sufficient to cast off a core belief, namely, the whole notion of a divine providence actively and beneficially engaged in

Irenaeus of Lyon

human affairs. So writes the outstanding empiricist philosopher of this period, John Stuart Mill (1806-1873): 'Not even on the most distorted and contracted theory of good which ever was framed by religious or philosophical fanaticism, can the government of Nature be made to resemble the work of a being at once good and omnipotent'. Two decades later Mill's godson, Bertrand Russell (1872-1970), arguably the most high profile atheist of the twentieth century, was to echo Shelley's words: 'My own view on religion is that of Lucretius. I regard it as a disease born of fear and as a source of untold misery to the human race'.[17]

We have already considered the first major theodicy to attempt a resolution of the problem – the Free Will Defence – and have found this inadequate for a number of reasons, not least because it still leaves God implicated in the sufferings of humanity, either directly in the case of non-moral evil or indirectly in the case of moral evil. Let us turn now to the second great theodicy. Borrowing a phrase from the poet John Keats, this is usually called the Argument from Soul-Making. The principal contemporary exponent of this theodicy is the English philosopher and theologian John Hick (1922-2012), but the argument is an ancient one and looks back to the work of Irenaeus of Lyon (c.135-140-c.202), first Bishop of Lyons, and the most important theologian of the second century.

---

16 *Lectures and Essays*, New York, Macmillan, 1901, pp.163-176. Reprinted in *The Ethics of Belief Debate*, ed. Gerald D. McCarthy, Atlanta, Georgia, Scholars Press, 1986, pp.19-24.

17 'Has Religion made useful Contributions to Civilisation? (1930). Reprinted in *Why I am not a Christian*, London, George Allen & Unwin, 1975, p.27.

John Hick

Irenaeus' argument is invariably presented as the great alternative to Augustine's theodicy. Although sharing with Augustine the view that evil occurs through the agency of human free will, Irenaeus argues that God, in choosing not to create a perfect world, requires imperfect man to struggle towards the finite 'likeness' of God. Instead of Augustine's doctrine that man incomprehensibly destroys his own created perfection – evil thus presenting a disruption of the divine plan – Irenaeus pictures man in the process of creation, as an initially immature creature seeking moral growth. Accordingly God is implicated in the sufferings of the world: in enabling man to be free, God permits evil to occur as a necessary part of the environment in which moral maturity can be achieved.

In his classic study of the problem of evil – *Evil and the God of Love* (1966) – Hick's position emerges as an elaboration of Irenaean theodicy. The essential premise of his argument is that it was never part of the divine plan to create human beings in a state of perfection, as end-states existing in a paradise from which, according to the mythology of the Fall, they disastrously fell away. Rather, God's purpose was more teleological and developmental: to create individuals 'in process of becoming the perfected being whom God is seeking to create'.[18] This progressive process, however, without which no spiritual or moral growth would be possible, is fraught with difficulties and dangers; and it is an environment in which the experience of suffering is an indispensable ingredient of the 'soul-making' enterprise, even to the point where, as Hick acknowledges, it can undermine religious belief altogether. But even this possible denial of God is part of God's plan: God is here deliberately hiding himself, creating an 'epistemic distance' between himself and individuals and refraining from giving too much knowledge of himself for fear that it would endanger the development of 'authentic fiduciary attitudes', in which individuals come to know God not out of necessity but freely. To the criticism (voiced already by Hume) that the amount of evil in experience far exceeds anything rationally required for such a programme, Hick employs his 'counterfactual

18 *Op.cit.*, Edition used, London, The Fontana Library, 1974, p.292.

hypothesis' or 'negative theodicy'. What would an 'hedonic paradise' be like? We can certainly imagine such a world: a world in which all possibility of pain and suffering is excluded, where no injuries are sustained, no crimes committed, no lies told or individuals betrayed. But it would also be a world bereft of any distinction between right and wrong, devoid of any wrong actions or any right actions in distinction from wrong. Indeed, it would be the worst of all possible worlds, converting a person-making environment into an uncreative and static one, in which moral attributes, such as generosity, kindness, courage and love, would have no place. If, to use the familiar analogy, God is to be represented as a Heavenly Father, wishing the best for his children, then this environment, in which pleasure becomes the sole value, cannot be the one best suited for the development of the most valuable potentialities of human personality.

> It think it is clear that a parent who loves his children, and wants them to become the best human beings that they are capable of becoming, does not treat pleasure as the sole or supreme value. Certainly we seek pleasure for our children, and take great delight in obtaining it for them; but we do not desire for them unalloyed pleasure at the expense of their growth in such even greater values as moral integrity, unselfishness, compassion, courage, humour, reverence for the truth, and perhaps above all the capacity for love. We do not act on the premise that pleasure is the supreme end of life; and if the development of these other values sometimes clashes with the provision of pleasure, then we are willing to have our children miss a certain amount of this, rather than fail to come to possess and to be possessed by the finer and more precious qualities that are possible to the human personality. A child brought up on the principle that the only or the supreme value is pleasure would not be likely to become an ethically mature adult or an attractive or happy personality. And to most parents it seems more important to try to foster quality and strength of character in their children than to fill their lives at all times with the utmost degree of pleasure. If, then, there is any true analogy between God's purpose for his human creatures, and the purpose of loving and wise parents for their children, we have to recognize that the presence of pleasure and the absence of pain cannot be the supreme and overriding end for which the world exists. Rather, this world must be a place of soul-making. And its value is to be judged, not primarily by the quantity of pleasure and pain occurring in it at any particular moment, but by its fitness for its primary purpose, the purpose of soul-making.[19]

---

19 *Ibid.*, p.295.

J.S. Mill

Hick's argument is a major attempt to resolve the problem of evil; and it is worth mentioning that *The Encyclopedia of Unbelief*, which is understandably fairly dismissive of modern theology, praises Hick for his intellectual honesty and for providing the most formidable theodicy to date.[20] But it remains unsuccessful nonetheless, as, I hope, the following points will make clear. Hick's suggestion is that God's world has been in part designed for educational purposes, the aim here being the improvement of the moral and spiritual health of the individual, a programme which would have no meaning in an hedonistic paradise devoid of any moral values. Given, however, that this educational device applies both to those who are spiritually healthy and unhealthy – that the bubonic plague does not discriminate – the application of suffering as an educational tool seems haphazard, to say the least, with no attempt being made to make the pain appropriate to the case at hand, to adjust the lesson to those who most need it. Indeed, there are some who appear to require no lessons at all, whose ease of life is presumably ill-adapted for any moral improvement. Nor indeed does the lesson seem appropriate to those incapable of learning anything at all. Given that the gorilla or the infant cannot appreciate the moral virtues like courage and self-sacrifice, it seems unfair that they should nevertheless have to undergo the sufferings which have proved so efficacious for the soul-making of others. In other words, if this is God's design, then it seems remarkably weighted against those who, through no fault of their own, are destined to learn no lessons through the pain they experience, who cannot turn to God because God is unknown to them. It also seems weighted against those with little time to spare for their education. People die young, with no chance to experience the full range of situations upon which

---

20 *Op.cit.*, p.191. The entry article on Evil is written by a well-known critic of Hick, Peter H. Hare, who here duplicates the arguments already presented in 'A Critique of Hick's Theodicy', co-authored with Edward H. Madden, in *Evil and The Concept of God*, Springfield. Illinois, Charles C. Thomas, 1968, pp.83-90, 102-103.

their moral development depends. However, the most serious objection to Hick's proposal concerns the fact of 'dysteleological suffering', i.e., excessive pain, pain that is out of all proportion to any benefits that may accrue. In many cases, the suffering endured is so great that it does not edify but crushes the personality completely. Here evil does not result in good but in further evil. This point is made much of by John Stuart Mill (1806-1873), the outstanding representative of the empirical and liberal traditions of Victorian England.

> . . . both good and evil naturally tend to fructify, each in its own kind, good producing good, and evil, evil. It is one of Nature's general rules, and part of her habitual injustice, that "to him that hath shall be given, but from him that hath not, shall be taken even that which he hath." The ordinary and predominant tendency of good is towards more good. Health, strength, wealth, knowledge, virtue, are not only good in themselves but facilitate and promote the acquisition of good, both of the same and of other kinds. The person who can learn easily, is he who already knows much: it is the strong and not the sickly person who can do everything which most conduces to health; those who find it easy to gain money are not the poor but the rich; while health, strength, knowledge, talents, are all means of acquiring riches, and riches are often an indispensable means of acquiring these. Again, *e converso*, whatever may be said of evil turning into good, the general tendency of evil is towards further evil. Bodily illness renders the body more susceptible of disease; it produces incapacity of exertion, sometimes debility of mind, and often the loss of means of subsistence. All severe pain, either bodily or mental, tends to increase the susceptibilities of pain for ever after. Poverty is the parent of a thousand mental and moral evils. What is still worse, to be injured or oppressed, when habitual, lowers the whole tone of the character. One bad action leads to others, both in the agent himself, in the bystanders, and in the sufferers. All bad qualities are strengthened by habit, and all vices and follies tend to spread. Intellectual defects generate moral, and moral, intellectual; and every intellectual or moral defect generates others, and so on without end.[21]

It would appear, then, that God's omniscience does not extend to a more precise calculation of where to draw the line, of 'fine-tuning' the dosage to achieve the best possible result. Once again, it is all a question

---

21 'Nature'. *Three Essays on Religion* (1874). For a modern edition, see Bristol, Thoemmes Press, 1993, pp.23-59. Also *TAC*: 161-174.

of degree. In the specific case of a child dying of cerebral meningitis, one must doubt whether the moral effects produced, such as sympathy for the cries of the child or for the anguish of the parents, could ever justify why the disease is there in the first place or why medical science should have so conspicuously failed to prevent it. It would be devilish to consider the moral gain sufficient compensation for the lack of treatment, and it is highly unlikely that any doctor, however philosophically inclined, would make this point to a bereaved mother. It may be, of course, that in these particularly harrowing cases, where the individual is simply overwhelmed by the pain he or she is experiencing, a divine plan is evident in the 'epistemic distance' it creates, even to the point that God is denied. Hick is clear that human beings are not to be made unambiguously aware of God's overpowering presence, which would place them in a kind of cognitive straightjacket, stifling freewill. But if this is so, the plan can hardly be considered a total success. Freedom and faith are here built on the back of God keeping himself very much to himself, of remaining hidden until certain individuals overcome their ignorance and come to believe. And this is undoubtedly the case for some. But for other individuals the hiddenness of God remains absolute, the excessive pain inflicted upon them obliterating any possibility that an omnipotent and benevolent God exists. Why God should have allowed this to happen is hard to see. Why did he not make himself better known to those in such distress, and thereby alleviate, if only in small measure, their suffering by at least giving some point to it by placing their experience within some kind of divine perspective? His failure to do this only makes his desire for anonymity inexcusable; and those who suffer can hardly be blamed for regarding their pain as being, after all, pointless, as bringing no benefit, and as providing thereby incontrovertible evidence that no good God exists. For why believe in a God as heartless as this?

Criticisms such as these have been widely canvassed, and Hick is well aware of them. Moreover, it is perhaps because he recognizes their force that, in the end, he takes refuge by appealing to 'mystery': the mystery, he writes, 'of dysteleological suffering is a real mystery, impenetrable to the rationalizing mind'.[22] For one of Hick's critics, this remark smacks of surrender. 'Does one not detect', asks Roland Puccetti, 'a small white flag waving in the smoke there'.[23] Certainly this retreat into mystery resolves nothing but rather reduces the question before us – of why innocent and excessive suffering exists in God's world – to a question

---

22 Op.cit., p.371.

23 'The Loving God: Some Observations on Hick's Theodicy', The Problem of Evil, ed. Michael Peterson, Notre Dame, Indiana, University of Notre Dame Press, 1992, p. 243.

with no discernible answer: a conclusion which leaves the field to the atheist. For if the answer, if answer there be, is indeed incomprehensible to the rationalizing mind, then it is hardly worth the asking, given that it will be unintelligible to those who asked the question. Putting the question thereby becomes no more than a rhetorical device. Thus against the evidential argument from evil the inscrutability of God is hardly the card to play. For this is not an explanation but an admission that no explanation will ever be forthcoming, or rather, that if it ever is we shall never understand it. In the absence of any confirming theistic explanation, the disconfirming atheistic explanation therefore stands alone; and in consequence the existence of suffering remains for many the decisive and unanswerable objection to the existence of God.

5
Morality and Religion

i. Introduction

In a letter to N.L. Ozmidov, in 1878, Fyodor Dostoevsky writes:

> Now assume there is no God or immortality of the soul. Now tell me, why should I live righteously and do good deeds if I am to die entirely on earth? And if that is so, why shouldn't I (as long as I can rely on my cleverness and agility to avoid being caught by the law) cut another man's throat, rob, and steal . . .[1]

Dostoevsky deploys this argument elsewhere in his novels. In *The Brothers Karamazov* (1880), Ivan Karamazov remarks that 'if there is no God, then everything is permitted'. Sometimes known, therefore, as the 'Karamazov defence', this line of argument is a familiar one in theistic apologetics, deriving a good deal of its strength from its simplicity. There are, so the argument runs, certain universal moral truths which have a normative value in our day to day living: e.g., that lying and murdering people are intrinsically wrong and that keeping one's promises and defending the innocent are intrinsically right. These truths are not, in other words, provisional, to be adopted solely at our convenience, when they advance our own particular goals or ends: rather, they are categorical, determining what we 'ought' to do irrespective of our situation or personal inclinations. These moral truths, we may say, have an *objective* rather than *subjective* status, and are in this respect more akin to *moral facts*, which it is our moral duty to uphold and live by. The question then arises: how are we best to explain the objectivity of these moral laws? For the believer the answer lies with the presumption that God exists. It is God's existence alone that can sustain the existence of absolute moral truths. Thus:

1 If absolute moral laws exist, then God exists.
2 Absolute moral laws exist.
3 Therefore God exists.

---

1   *Selected Letters of Fyodor Dostoyevsky*, edited Joseph Frank and David Goldstein, New Brunswick, Rutgers University Press, 1987, p.446.

The Karamazov defence carries with it an additional argument. It is not merely that without God there can be no objective moral standards – a conclusion which supposes that, in all probability, without these standards the world would relapse into a kind of moral anarchy – but also that without God there is no binding *motive* to be good. In other words, it is part of the categorical structure of a universal moral truth that it should be binding upon the individual, and this would not be the case if breaches of the law went unpunished. Atheists,

Fyodor Dostoevsky

therefore, being without any belief in divine punishment for such offences, feel no compulsion to obey. It is on these grounds that the English philosopher, John Locke (1632-1704), in his *Letter Concerning Toleration* (1689), refuses toleration to those 'who deny the being of God' because 'Promises, covenants, and oaths, which are the bonds of human society, can have no hold upon an atheist'.[2] This is not to say, of course, that the civil authorities, through the institutions of justice, do not successfully punish wrongdoers; but these cannot provide any guarantee of success – criminals, after all, are not always convicted and crime frequently pays. It is only therefore by believing in a divine and omniscient justice that one can be assured that justice will inevitably be done. If not in this life then in the next a system of divine rewards and punishments will operate, which the law-breaker cannot avoid and by which he will be certainly condemned.

I should add here that, while this belief in Life after Death is frequently twinned with the belief that God is the presupposition of the moral law, this is not a *logical* connection, that the one cannot be understood without the other. For there is no contradiction in claiming either that there is a God but no post-mortem existence, as Voltaire argued, or

---

2   Ed. Charles Sherman, New York, Appleton-Centry, 1937, pp.212-213. A view shared by George Bush, Snr. In answer to the question put to him by the reporter Robert Sherman 'Surely you recognize the equal citizenship and patriotism of Americans who are atheists?' Bush replied, 'No. I don't know that atheists should be considered as citizens, nor should they be considered patriots. This is one nation under God'. O'Hare Airport, Chicago, Illinois, 27 August, 1987.

that there is immortality but no God, an exclusion found in the belief in reincarnation or survival as rebirth. In both these cases the idea of a divine justice, impelling obedience to the moral law, does not apply. More importantly, however, even distinguished theists, with their ideas of immortality intact, have not subscribed to the moral argument for God. Thomas Aquinas (c.1225-1274), for example, did not include it among the many arguments he provided for God's existence.[3] For him an unchangeable and universal moral truth was not unlike a truth of logic and mathematics, and therefore human beings could act morally irrespective of whether a God exists or not. Much later Gottfried Leibniz (1646-1716), although providing a famous theodicy to defend God's perfection,[4] rejects the argument in a way that prefigures many modern criticisms. The argument, he contends, replaces the notion of a loving God with an autocratic deity, whose every whim must be right.

> Also, if we say that things are good by no rule of goodness beyond the will of God alone, we thoughtlessly destroy, I feel, all the love and glory of God. For why praise Him for what He had done if He would be equally praiseworthy for doing the opposite? Where will His justice and His wisdom be, if all that remains of Him is some kind of despotic power. If His will takes the place of reason, and if, by the very definition of tyranny, what pleases the Almighty is *ipso facto* just?[5]

While it undoubtedly helps the atheist's case that believers are themselves divided on the issue, the fact remains that the moral argument for God's existence is for many a stalwart of their belief, with a distinguished pedigree. I have already mentioned Locke, but other supporters include the medieval theologian Duns Scotus (c.1226-1308), the great Reformation figures of Martin Luther (1483-1546) and John Calvin (1509-1564), Locke's contemporary George Berkeley (1685-1753), and perhaps surprisingly, given his criticisms of the theistic proofs, Immanuel Kant (1724-1804).[6] More recently other variants have been forthcoming. The most popular and widely-read modern advocate is undoubtedly C.S. Lewis (1898-1963), who gave a classic account of it in his *Mere Christianity* (1952). According to Lewis, there is something

---

3   See above, p.37

4   See above, pp.56-59

5   *Discourse on Metaphysics* (1686), edited and translated with an Introduction and glossary by R.N.D. Martin and Stuart Brown, Manchester and New York, Manchester University Press, 1988, p.40.

6   Kant's defence of the moral argument is the most influential of all but alas! sufficiently complicated to be omitted here. I examine it at length in my *QG*: 235-250.

over and above our observations of the natural world, something 'which is directing the universe, and which appears to me as a law urging me to do right and making me feel responsible and uncomfortable when I do wrong'.[7] More recently this type of argument has gone under the general heading of *divine command theory*. This, as its name suggests, has concentrated more on God's role as authoritative 'legislator' of the moral law. Another variant is the idea that God acts as a 'commander', that it is by divine command that moral action will be deemed good, thereby requiring unconditional obedience on the part of the moral agents. These later variants have raised the profile of the moral argument to the point where atheists must once again address themselves to the plausibility of God as sole moral arbiter.

ii. Criticisms of the Moral Argument

However, of all the arguments for God's existence the moral argument is the weakest, causing atheists little trouble. This is not least because, as we have just noted, many believers themselves agree that the argument should be discarded. But even from the outset, the absurdities of the argument become apparent. For if it is the case that moral values depend on God's existence, then believers are in the somewhat embarrassing position of having to agree that distinguished atheists of the stature of Lucretius, Spinoza, Mill, Hume, George Eliot, Einstein and Russell were somehow on a lower plane of moral awareness than the most commonplace believers, the latter being tapped into the only true vein of righteous behaviour – a conclusion which is, frankly, hard to stomach. But that is not all. For the moral argument to succeed it will be necessary for adherents to show that *any* secular theory of morality – one which assigns moral responsibility to unbelievers and which thus accepts their non-religious moral values as legitimate – will be somehow intellectually deficient and must therefore defer to the religious alternative. But this too is hard to take. In the history of philosophy there have been many theories of morality that claim that absolute moral laws can be generated without presuming God's existence. 'That there is a God' is certainly one explanation of why we share certain moral values; but it competes with many others, less metaphysically ambitious. It is quite possible, for example, to delete the theistic overtones of Kantian theory, and say that certain moral absolutes can be generated through the mechanism of the categorical imperative alone; or with Thomas Hobbes to maintain that such absolutes proceed from an entirely selfish motive, which is to protect citizens both from themselves and from an otherwise brutish state of nature. Evolutionists, on the other hand, have argued that moral

7   London, Fontana Books, 1964, pp.33.

rules create a stable environment in which to rear vigorous individuals, so increasing their chances of survival. These, then, are just three of the many theories that could be catalogued here, all of them subscribing to the view that morality can have an objective basis without religion.[8] The task before the believer is thus a daunting one. For it is precisely these systems of ethics, formulated without reference to God, that religious moralists must show to be unsuccessful if their argument is to be successful. But, as yet, no comprehensive critique of these many alternatives has been forthcoming.

Turning now to the specifics of the theistic case, the following four philosophical objections may be listed:

1 The most important criticism derives from a question first put by Socrates in the Platonic dialogue Euthyphro. Euthyphro is a young theologian bringing a case against his father, whom he alleges has murdered a labourer on Euthryphro's estate at Naxos: this, the young man states, is the 'holy' thing to do. In response to Socrates' irritating questions, Euthyphro further defines 'Holiness' as 'what the gods all love, and its opposite is what the gods all hate, unholiness'.[9] To this Socrates asks the decisive question: 'Is what is holy, holy because the gods approve of it, or do they approve of it because it is holy?'[10] Socrates' question may be formulated as follows:

Either: a right act is right because God approves (or commands) it; *Or*: God approves (or commands) a right action because it is right.

This alternative clarifies the problem for the believer. For while the first option presupposes God's existence as the foundation of moral action – that 'If God wills X, X is right' – the second clearly does not. This is not to say that God does not exist, but rather that 'X is right' is *first* independently validated as being good, and *then* applied to God as a command worthy of him. It is not so much, then, that nothing is morally wrong unless God has forbidden it, but rather that God would not forbid anything that was not morally wrong – i.e., that what he forbids depends on some *prior standard of goodness*. However, having

---

8   Michael Martin has paid particular attention to two modern theories – the Ideal Observer Theory developed by C.D. Broad, Roderick Firth and William Frankena and others; and the method of Wide Reflective Equilibrium, developed by Nelson Goodman, John Rawls and others. See *Atheism, Morality and Meaning*, Amherst, New York, Prometheus Books, 2002, pp.49-110.

9   *Plato: The Collected Dialogues*, ed. Edith Hamilton and Huntingdon Cairns, trans. Lane Cooper, Bollingen Series 71, New York, Pantheon Books, 1966, p.174.

10 *Ibid.*, p.178.

this independent standard of judgement means that deciding whether an action is right or wrong requires no appeal to theistic premises, and that, accordingly, God's existence makes no difference to the moral situation.

Socrates

2 This criticism reduces divine command theory to the level of a tautology. If it is not the case, as we have just seen, that 'God commands X *because* X is good', then the alternative is 'Whatever X is, it will be good if God commands it', the good here being defined by the divine command. This reduces 'God commands what is good' to the uninformative 'God commands what God commands', thus making the question '*Ought* I to obey what God commands?' morally redundant. For I cannot ask whether I ought to obey God when what God orders is good by definition.

3 But if what God orders is by definition good, then another difficulty arises: whether an action is regarded as right or wrong is now entirely arbitrary, depending on divine whim. If God decides that we should slaughter a hostile tribe, with thirty thousand virgins as our reward – as he does in the Old Testament book of *Numbers*, Chapter 31 – then that action is right because God commands it. If, however, we view this command as ethically reprehensible, then we have in effect abandoned the idea that *whatever* God commands is right, and have evaluated this particular command by our own rational criteria about what is the morally right thing to do, and have concluded that wholesale murder and rape can never be elevated to the status of a moral duty. In this case, then, disobeying God cannot be wrong, and *not* doing what God orders is right. This too invalidates the claim that what God orders is right.

The atheistic literature, we should add, is full of biblical examples similar to the one just given, in which atrocities are condoned because sanctioned by God, so legitimating murder, rape, plunder, torture, slavery, genocide and ethnic cleansing. This makes it difficult to resist the

Bertrand Russell

conclusion that the God of the Jews and Christians is, to quote the American radical Elihu Palmer (1764-1806), 'a changeable, passionate, angry, unjust, and revengeful being; infuriate in his wrath, capricious in his conduct, and destitute, in many respects, of those sublime and immutable properties which really belong to the Preserver of the universe'.[11] It is customary at this point, when the biblical record becomes ethically suspect, to make a distinction not just between the Old and New Testaments but also between the respective roles of Jesus and of his more ruthlessly eager followers. This allows the faithful, at any rate, to exonerate Jesus from responsibility for the Church's often lamentable history of cruelty and injustice. Many atheists, however, are unhappy even with this convention, and have maintained that there were flaws both in the personality and in the teaching of Jesus of Nazareth, and that it was these defects which have had such a noxious influence on the moral standing of the Church. As an example of this type of *ad hominem* criticism none better can be found than Bertrand Russell's highly influential *Why I am not a Christian*, a lecture first delivered in 1927 and included in the collection of essays published under the same title in 1957.

> There is one very serious defect to my mind in Christ's moral character, and that is that He believed in hell. I do not myself feel that any person who is really profoundly humane can believe in everlasting punishment. Christ certainly as depicted in the Gospels did believe in everlasting punishment, and one does find repeatedly a vindictive fury against those people who would not listen to His preaching – an attitude which is not uncommon

11 Quoted in *Varieties of Unbelief*, edited J.C.A. Gaskin, New York & London, Macmillan, 1989, p.109. A comprehensive list of biblical atrocities is provided by Elizabeth Anderson in 'If God is Dead, is Everything Permitted?' in *Philosophers Without God*, edited L.M. Anthony, Oxford, Oxford University Press, 2007, pp.215-230.

with preachers, but which does somewhat detract from superlative excellence. You do not, for instance find that attitude in Socrates. . . . There is, of course, the familiar text about the sin against the Holy Ghost: 'Whosoever speaketh against the Holy Ghost it shall not be forgiven him neither in this World nor in the world to come.' That text has caused an unspeakable amount of misery in the world, for all sorts of people have imagined that they have committed the sin against the Holy Ghost, and thought that it would not be forgiven them either in this world or in the world to come. I really do not think that a person with a proper degree of kindliness in his nature would have put fears and terrors of that sort into the world. . . . Then He says again, 'If thy hand offend thee, cut it off; it is better for thee to enter into life maimed, than having two hands to go into Hell, into the fire that never shall be quenched; where the worm dieth not and the fire is not quenched.' He repeats that again and again also. I must say that I think all this doctrine, that hell-fire is a punishment for sin, is a doctrine of cruelty. It is a doctrine that put cruelty into the world and gave the world generations of cruel torture; and the Christ of the Gospels, if you could take Him as His chroniclers represent Him, would certainly have to be considered partly responsible for that.[12]

4 It might be argued, of course, that many of the scenarios just presented are entirely fanciful, and that a 'loving God' would never order the faithful to murder or rape. The believer could thus exclude certain commands as not as coming from God at all, as being entirely contrary to what he or she regards as God's true nature, as being not of divine but of demonic origin. Thus the believer could offer very good reasons for disputing whether a reported command of God does indeed come from God: it may not, for example, conform to certain passages of scripture or to what the Church ordains, and so on. But this argument in fact resolves nothing. The moral agent is here freely and autonomously deciding whether to obey a particular command or not, and a particular action – to kill the innocent – has been here excluded *on other grounds* than that God commanded it. For once again the decision to obey (or not) has been *preceded* by an independent evaluation of whether this command is good (or not), the conclusion being that this is an evil command, and something therefore that God would forbid and not command. But here again we have employed a *prior* standard of goodness in deciding what acts to attribute to God,

12 Ed. Paul Edwards, George Allen & Unwin, 1957, pp.18-27. See also *TAC*: 207-208.

one which invalidates the claim that what God ordains is necessarily
good. For we must now admit that there are other reasons for saying
that a certain moral action is or is not worthy of God; and that it is
these reasons, independently reached, which inform us whether or nor
this action ought to be performed. Thus in the moment that we credit
goodness *to* God we invalidate any argument that goodness comes
from God alone.

iii. Life after Death and Morality

The conclusion that absolute moral rules may exist without God existing
does not, of course, invalidate the subsidiary religious claim that there
is a greater likelihood that these rules will be upheld if there is a post-
mortem system of rewards and punishments administered by an all-
seeing deity. Even if we set aside at this point the atheist's more usual
claim that there is absolutely no reliable empirical evidence to suggest
that human beings do in fact achieve some kind of immortality and that,
moreover, there are perfectly reasonable psychological explanations for
why they should believe that they do – a claim that I shall refer to in a
later chapter[13] – there yet remains something deeply problematic about
the idea that human beings are better motivated to act righteously during
life if they know that they will somehow be called to account after death.

It is part of the theistic case that moral commands generated by
a naturalistic ethics remain moored to diverse cultural and social
environments, and that accordingly there can be no absolute moral
values: what may be reprehensible in one society may not be in another.
We are told, however, that in the religious tradition the situation is very
different. God's commands may, for example, be communicated directly
to the faithful through scriptural revelation (e.g., the Bible or Koran), or
through the commands handed down by great religious figures (Jesus or
Mohammad); and that people will be subsequently judged according to
whether they have or have not obeyed these clear moral objectives. But
here, too, the religious alternative fails to satisfy, if only because these
moral objectives are anything but clear when put into practice. So while
the moral prohibition against taking life explains the pacifism of the
Quakers, the same command has not prevented other Christian groups
from arguing that killing is justified in war or in defence of the innocent.
The same religious tradition may therefore generate different moral
positions – a fact which certainly weakens the claim that it is only here, and
not within the variabilities of secular morality, that access can be gained
to an authoritative and divinely revealed truth, with rich rewards for the
obedient. Indeed, going further, we can say that for every moral truth that

---

13 See below, pp.130-156

religion A practically applies, the logical possibility remains that religion B will condemn it, and that any practical application that religion B commends will be condemned by another religion (C) and so on. Thus for every religion requiring one course of action, and threatening all others, there is another actual or possible religion threatening that course of action and rewarding all others. It is, of course, also logically possible that only one religion is in fact the true religion, and that is only here that benefits are

Blaise Pascal

awarded; but quite which religion this is will be impossible to say, given that we have now generated an infinite number of logically possible religions.

If, then, the religious criticism of secular ethics is that it contains no one authoritative source of morality, then much the same can be said by the atheist of religious ethics. And to these difficulties we may add another. We are told that the prospect of rewards and punishment after death reinforces the motive to do good while alive, and that from a purely pragmatic point of view it makes no sense to forgo a life of infinite and heavenly bliss for the sake of immediate and earthly pleasures. This juxtaposition is central to the famous Wager of Blaise Pascal (1623-1662), who advised the potential believer to act prudently, and to place his bet on God existing rather than not, if only because here the pay-off is so much greater. After all, if one bets against God and no God exists, no harm is done; but if one bets against God and God does exist, the consequences for the gambler could be dire. This, after all, is a game of chance in which there could not be a higher pay-off, where there is 'an infinity of infinitely happy life to be won'.[14]

For the famous twentieth-century English philosopher, G.E. Moore (1873-1958), Pascal's Wager was 'absolutely wicked',[15] and one can certainly see why. For not only does it assume that God is revengeful and

14 *Pensées*, edited and translated by A.J. Krailsheimer, London & New York, Penguin Books, p.151

15 Quoted by Paul Levy, *Moore*, London, Weidenfeld & Nicolson, p. 214

not all-forgiving – an assumption that many believers themselves reject – it also converts faith into a thoroughly mercenary activity, morally reprehensible through cold-blooded calculation. Nor is it at all obvious that God would prefer to reward believers motivated by self-interest rather than those atheists who have set aside any profit-incentives in favour of a higher moral obligation, namely, not to believe anything on insufficient evidence. And for all we know, an omniscient God, looking into the hearts of men, may prefer the so-called 'immoral atheist' to the 'moral theist'. Perhaps, therefore, when all is said and done, honesty may remain the best policy, and a wager against God may turn out to be prudentially the better bet, offering a reward that might be denied to self-serving believers. One is here reminded of the following conversation presented by the editor of the *L'Encyclopédie*, the *philosophe* Denis Diderot (1713-1784) between Mme La Maréchale and Crudeli:

L.M.:   Are you not Monsieur Crudeli?
Crudeli: Yes, madame.
L.M.:   The man who believes in nothing?
Crudeli: I am.
L.M.:   But your morals are the same as a believer's?
Crudeli: Why not, if that believer is an honest man?
L.M.:   And do you put that morality into practice?
Crudeli: As well as I can.
L.M.:   What! you do not steal, or kill, or pillage?
Crudeli: Very rarely.
L.M.:   Then what do you get out of not believing?
Crudeli: Nothing; but does one believe in order to get something out of it?[16]

Unsurprisingly, then, the moral argument for God has not fared well among the great majority of contemporary philosophers, and for very good reasons. In the first place the claim that God is the foundation of the moral life begs the question not merely of whether any God exists but whether this God does indeed have the characteristics that faith ascribes to him: whether, for example, he is an avenging God or not or whether he would in an after-life mete out justice to unbelievers and reward the faithful. If this cannot be demonstrated, then it is hard to resist the conclusion that the reasoning employed by the moral argument has become entirely circular and so fallacious. The existence of an objective law is first used to establish the first premise of the argument – that there is a God – and this self-same first premise is then employed to establish a conclusion, namely, that without God's

---

16 'Conversations with a Christian Lady' (1774), *Diderot's Selected Writings*, New York, Macmillan, 1966, p.253.

existence there could be no objective law. I am not alone, therefore, in concluding that there is absolutely no mileage in this argument: a conclusion pointed out by, among many others, J.L. Mackie (1982), James Rachels (1971), Robin Le Poidevin (1996), Michael Martin (2002), Anthony Grayling (2003), and, most prominently of all, Kai Nielsen. [17] For Nielsen a humanistic world-view is implicit in each person's pattern of moral action and moral choice; and while a naturalistic ethics lacks the fundamental orientation towards a belief in a teleological creation – that there is some overarching purpose to life – this does not imply that no purpose can be achieved *in* life, that there can be no moral aims in a godless world. For moral atheists may also have their ambitions – not least to reduce human pain and suffering and to foster happiness, love, comradeship and fraternity – and these, indeed, are commitments invariably shared by the believer.

> If you have some life plan, if you want to be a doctor or a professor or a political radical, whatever you want to be, if there's something you want to do in this world, you can do that, God or no God. There are all those intentions, purposes, goals, and the like that you can figure out and find and can have. They are what John Rawls called *life plans*. You figure out what you want to do with your life. You can have all these purposes *in* life even though there is no purpose *to* life, so life doesn't become meaningless and pointless if you were not *made for* a purpose.
>
> There can be small individual purposes, things like love, friendship, caring, knowledge, self-respect, pleasure in life. All of these things remain perfectly intact in a godless world. There can also be larger political and social purposes that you can struggle for. You can, in Camus's famous phrase, fight the plague, if you will. Even if you are skeptical about transforming the world, at least you can try to cut back some of the evil in the world, and sometimes you can succeed in some measure.
>
> And all of this remains perfectly in place in a godless universe. You don't have to have a Kierkegaardian sense of sickness unto death where all worldly hopes are undermined because there is no purpose to life. There are these intact purposes in life, and

17 See John Mackie, *The Miracle of Theism*, Oxford, Clarendon Press, 1982, pp.102-118; James Rachels, 'God and Human Attitudes,' reprinted in *Divine Commands and Morality*, ed. Paul Helm, Oxford, Oxford University Press, 1981, pp.34-48; Robin Le Poidevin, *Arguing for Atheism*, London & New York, Routledge, 1996, pp.73-87; Michael Martin, *Atheism, Morality and Meaning*, Buffalo, New York, Prometheus Books, 2002; Anthony Grayling, *What is Good?* London, Weidenfeld & Nicolson, 2003, pp.59-63.

they can be forged together in clusters to give you a coherent but still utterly secularist worldview. There are, that is, things that are worthwhile doing and having. It is worthwhile struggling to make a better world. Friendship, love, caring, all these things I mentioned remain intact in a godless world.[18]

The fact, then, that there are moral values that are shared by both theists and atheists – that God or no God, there are moral values that remain intact with or without a religious belief – makes two things clear: first, that believers must demonstrate not merely that they have an additional and superior moral reason for their behaviour, but that this reason in some way makes a substantive difference to the day-to-day practice of morality; and second, that atheists, being persuaded that no such reason will ever be forthcoming, can agree that morality has a rationale in complete independence of religion, and that accordingly the absence or loss of God makes absolutely no difference to the quality of the moral life they seek to pursue.

iv. Nietzsche's Critique of Religious Morality

In the literature of atheism, however, it is the critique of religious morality made by the German philosopher Friedrich Nietzsche (1844-1900) that stands apart. In terms of its literary style, dramatic character and sheer vitriol, no attack upon Christian ethics can equal it. I regard Nietzsche, along with Marx and Freud,[19] as the third member of the great triumvirate of atheism. The French philosopher Paul Ricoeur has called these three the pre-eminent 'philosophers of suspicion' – given that each of them, in their different ways, is suspicious of surface-meanings and seeks to unmask the fraudulent belief that the norms of culture and society are founded on infallible, universal truths.[20] In Nietzsche's case, the focus is upon the distorted vision of man presented primarily by Christianity, in which a corrupt ethic makes weakness both honourable and praiseworthy, which infects the natural flow of the 'will to power', and which in consequence has domesticated the individual to the point where his full potential can never be explored or ever realized. As he writes: 'That which defines me,

---

18 *Does God Exist?* (with J.P. Moreland), Buffalo, New York, Prometheus Books, 1993, pp.98-109. Nielsen has written extensively on the relation between God and morality. See also the following, all published by Prometheus Books at Buffalo, New York: *Philosophy and Atheism* (1985), *Why be Moral?* (1989), *Ethics Without God* (1990), *God and the Grounding of Morality* (1991). See also *TAC*: 210-220.

19 For extended discussions of Marx and Freud, see below, pp.133-156

20 *Freud and Philosophy: An Essay on Interpretation*, New Haven, Yale University Press, 1970, p.5

that which makes me stand apart from the whole of the rest of humanity, is the fact that I *unmasked* Christian morality.'[21]

Nietzsche's concerns are two-fold: the first critical, in standing as the strict adversary of Christian morality; the second positive, in seeking to provide an image of a new type of human being, one which is the antithesis of the Christian. These twin ambitions have as their backdrop Nietzsche's single most powerful and most publicized conviction that

Friedrich Nietzsche

'God is dead'. This assertion is made many times, but is best expressed in *The Gay Science* (1882), in the parable entitled 'The Madman'. I quote the passage in full:

> Have you not heard of that mad man who lit a lantern in the bright morning hours, ran to the market place, and cried incessantly, "I seek God! I seek God!" As many of those who did not believe in God were standing around just then, he provoked much laughter. Why, did he get lost? said one. Did he lose his way like a child? said another. Or is he hiding? Is he afraid of us? Has he gone on a voyage? or emigrated? Thus they yelled and laughed. The madman jumped into their midst and pierced them with his eyes. "Whither is God?" he cried. "I shall tell you. *We have killed him* – you and I. All of us are his murderers. But how have we done this? How were we able to drink up the sea? Who gave us the sponge to wipe away the entire horizon? What did we do when we unchained this earth from its sun? Whither is it moving now? Whither are we moving now? Away from all suns? Are we not plunging continually? Backward, sideward, forward, in all directions? Is there any up or down left? Are we not straying as through an infinite nothing? Do we not feel the breath of empty space? Has it not become colder? Is not night and more night coming on all the while? Must not lanterns be lit in the morning? Do we not hear anything yet of the noise of the grave-

21 *Ecce Homo*, translated, with an Introduction, by R.J. Hollingdale, Harmondsworth, Penguin Books, 1979, pp.131. A short selection of Nietzsche's writings are available at *TAC*: 220-239.

diggers who are burying God? Do we not smell anything yet of God's decomposition. Gods too decompose. God is dead. God remains dead. And we have killed him. How shall we, the murderers of all murderers, comfort ourselves? What was holiest and most powerful of all that the world has yet owned has bled to death under our knives. Who will wipe this blood off us? What water is there for us to clean ourselves? What festivals of atonement, what sacred games shall we have to invent? Is not the greatness of this deed too great for us? Must not we ourselves become gods simply to seem worthy of it? There has never been a greater deed; and whoever will be born after us – for the sake of this deed he will be part of a higher history than all history hitherto."

Here the madman fell silent and looked again at his listeners; and they, too, were silent and stared at him in astonishment. At last he threw his lantern on the ground, and it broke and went out. "I come too early," he said then; "my time is not yet. This tremendous event is still on its way, still wandering – it has not yet reached the ears of man. Lightning and thunder require time, the light of the stars requires time, deeds require time even after they are done, before they can be seen and heard. This deed is still more distant from them than the most distant stars – *and yet they have done it themselves*."

It has been related further that on that same day the madman forced his way into divers churches and there sang his *requiem aeternam deo*. Led out and called to account, he is said to have replied every time, "What are these churches now if they are not the tombs and sepulchers of God?"[22]

In this celebrated passage Nietzsche is describing not so much God's death but more exactly the death of the *belief* that a God exists. The statement that 'God is dead' (*Gott ist tot*) is not to be taken literally – that a being, once alive, has now died – but refers to a much more potent cultural fact: that human beings have turned away from God and no longer have any need of him as a source of moral value. Nor does this mean that God's death requires the death of belief, that the one is an implication of the other: one may, after all, still retain the fiction of God's existence despite the fact that there really *is* no God, an idea that has now been 'eliminated'. This point is made in the Introduction

---

22 Translated by Walter Kaufmann in *Existentialism from Dostoevsky to Sartre*, edited by Kaufmann, Cleveland & New York, The World Publishing Company, 1968, pp.105-106.

to Nietzsche's most famous book *Thus Spoke Zarathustra* (1883-1885), where the isolated saint, who spends his days singing God's praises, is unaware of this terrible truth: 'Could it be possible? This old saint in the forest has not yet heard anything of this, that *God is dead*'.[23] But for those who are aware of how things stand, or for those unaware but who must now be educated to the painful reality of their situation, the death of belief is an event of profound personal and social significance: their faith in a theocentric and providential universe that has sustained them for centuries must now be jettisoned. But for Nietzsche this provides a unique opportunity to discard once and for all the 'conceptual cobweb-spinning' of religion that has so impoverished our lives. God may be dead, and this may indeed be a verifiable fact of our civilization, but what must now be attempted is, as it were, to kill the beast off. This Nietzsche aims to achieve not just by exposing the tawdry nature of religious aspirations, so excising any *motivation* to believe, but also by undermining the appeal of making life endurable through the promise by religion of an after-life and immortality, which only serves to devalue and denigrate man's actual life through the fable of a judgment to come. This is the central drive behind Nietzsche's critical programme: that having exposed religion for what it is – and in particular the Christian religion – no return to a religious morality will be intellectually tenable or emotionally satisfying. That achieved, Nietzsche can then proceed to the second phase of his programme, to the positive enterprise. That is, to offer a 'revaluation of all values' or a 'higher morality' suitable only for a new kind of man, the *Übermensch* (the Overman), who operates 'beyond good and evil', and who gives meaning to life in a world no longer inhabited by God. In this respect, the *Übermensch* is not man's successor but God's. And with this usurpation of the place previously held by God, human beings can at last remove the principal obstacle to the development of strong and intellectually free individuals, and can finally break through the bonds of conventional morality and create their own values.

The force of Nietzsche's atheism can best be appreciated when he proceeds beyond the denial of God's existence to the denial of all those estimable characteristics traditionally associated with the Christian way of life. It is not enough to state that God is a 'failure of the intellect' and 'our most enduring lie'[24]. What is further required is to show how theistic belief was able to arise, how such a confusion of the mind

---

23 *Thus Spoke Zarathustra* in *The Portable Nietzsche*, translated, edited, with a critical introduction and notes by Walter Kaufmann, New York, Viking Press, 1969, p.124.

24 *The Gay Science* (1882), Nos. 151 & 344, translated by Walter Kaufmann, New York, Vintage Books, 1974.

could have acquired such weight and importance. How was it possible that Christianity could achieve such a success, so that qualities such as meekness, humility, self-denial, modesty, pity, compassion and denial of the flesh should be esteemed *virtues*, as part of the Christian ideal, when in fact they are no such thing but aspects of a creed that maims and debilitates life?

> I *condemn* Christianity. I raise against the Christian church the most terrible of all accusations that any accuser ever uttered. It is to me the highest of all conceivable corruptions . . .; it has turned every value into an un-value, every truth into a lie, every integrity into a vileness of the soul. . . . Parasitism as the *only* practice of the church; with its idea of anemia, all hope for life; the beyond as the will to negate every reality; the cross as the mark of recognition for the most subterranean conspiracy that ever existed – against health, beauty, whatever has turned out well, courage, spirit, *graciousness* of the soul, *against life itself.*[25]

In order to show how this process occurred, Nietzsche offers a quasi-historical survey of the origins of different moralities, the ancestry of which will reveal how the decadent ethics of religion, and of Christianity in particular, have arisen. Nietzsche's definitive description of this process is given in his *On the Genealogy of Morals* of 1887. Here he depicts two contrasting moralities. On the one hand is *noble morality*, with its key distinction between 'good and bad'; on the other is *slave morality*, with its core contrast between 'good and evil'. The *Genealogy* is for the most part concerned to show how the transition from the one to the other is effected. The idea that 'goodness' originates with those for whom goodness is useful, or to whom goodness is shown – i.e., the poor and dispossessed – is wrong. Rather, goodness is associated with everything that is 'noble', that is, with those who have the power to establish their actions *as* good by sheer force of will and privilege. The heroic and warrior qualities displayed by the aristocratic class are intelligence, courage, physical and mental strength, and pride. By contrast, 'bad' designates everything inferior that lacks these qualities, a social under-class, which possesses the opposite qualities of weakness, vulgarity, meanness etc. Nietzsche provides etymological warrants for this 'pathos of distance'. So the German *gut* is traced through to 'godlike', and the German for 'bad' (*schlecht*) is followed through to *schlicht*, standing here for the 'common man'.[26]

---

25 *The Anti-Christ* (written 1888, published 1895) in *The Portable Nietzsche*, ed. Kaufmann, p.655-656

26 From Nietzsche, Friedrich, *The Genealogy of Morals*, translated by Ian Johnston. Translation © Ian Johnston, 2009.

What we have here is an order of rank, with the noble type of man representing an ascending scale and the lower man a descending scale: these, as we shall soon discover, are not merely two social classes but rather two attitudes towards life. But how does the transition from noble to slave morality occur? This happens through 'the priestly mode of valuation'. The priests, motivated by the powerful emotion of *ressentiment*[27] towards their aristocratic superiors, canonize instead a value-system ascetic in character, far removed from the sensory and physical pleasures endorsed by the nobility. The classic embodiment of these values is Judaism. Fuelled by their hatred of those who are their natural oppressors, they take their revenge by a radical reversal of values, by converting the noble virtues of courage, self-confidence and intelligence into the vices of cruelty, arrogance and pride:

> In opposition to the aristocratic value equations (*good* = *noble* = *powerful* = *beautiful* = *fortunate* = *loved by god*), the Jews, with a consistency inspiring fear, dared to reverse things and to hang on to that with the teeth of the most profound hatred (the hatred of the powerless), that is, to 'only those who suffer are good; the poor, the powerless, the low are the only good people; the suffering, those in need, the sick, the ugly are also the only pious people; only they are blessed by God; for them alone there is salvation. – By contrast, you privileged and powerful people, you are for all eternity the evil, the cruel, the lecherous, the insatiable, the godless; you will also be the unblessed, the cursed, and the damned for all eternity!' . . . We know *who* inherited this Judaic transformation of values . . . with the Jews *the slave rebellion in morality begins*: that rebellion which has a two-thousand-year-old history behind it and which we nowadays no longer notice because it – has triumphed.[28]

There is little doubt about the identity of the morality pronounced victorious here. If one wants to know who has won this battle – the master or slave, Rome or Judaea – then the answer is clear:

> Just think of who it is people bow down to today in Rome itself as the personification of all the highest values – and not only in Rome, but in almost half the earth, all the places where people have become merely tame or want to become tame – in front

27 The French *ressentiment* is a key term in Nietzsche's philosophy and goes beyond the English 'resentment'. For while it retains the sense of bitterness towards stronger and more privileged individuals, Nietzsche's *ressentiment* generates *values*: the priests internalise and rationalise their weakness, and transform it into a morality that enslaves the strong.

28 *Ibid.*, 470.

of *three Jews*, as we know, and *one Jewess* (in front of Jesus of Nazareth, the fisherman Peter, the carpet maker Paul, and the mother of the first-mentioned Jesus, named Mary). This is very remarkable: without doubt Rome has been conquered.[29]

Nietzsche in army uniform

The exemplification of the slave revolt in morality (*der Sklavenaufstand in der Moral*) is Christianity, but the victory of Christianity is entirely ruinous for the development of the autonomous and life-embracing individual. With its gospel of self-denial and self-sacrifice Christianity places centre stage the attributes that slaves, as slaves, inevitably display before their masters – impotence, timidity, cowardice – and converts them into the virtues of humility, patience, friendliness and love of neighbour. Whereas the distinction between 'good and bad' in noble morality indicated an aristocratic indifference towards its social inferiors, the slave morality now applies the distinction 'good and *evil*' – the word 'evil' replacing 'bad' as an expression of its *ressentiment*, of its all-consuming hatred for all that is noblest and best. This revaluation of value is completed by looking at the world as a prison of vice from which it is necessary to escape, thereby promising salvation, through faith, in an invisible other world. Thus Christianity perpetuates 'the most fatal seductive lie that has yet existed. . . . I reject every compromise position with respect to it – I force war against it. Petty people's morality as the measure of things: this is the most disgusting degeneration culture has yet exhibited. And this kind of ideal still hanging over mankind is "God"!'[30]

It is tempting to see in Nietzsche's account of the dominance of Christian morality a reworking of Darwinian evolutionary theory, but here significantly reversed as the subjugation of the 'fittest' by the 'weak'. If the natural order of things were left intact, the struggle for survival

---

29 *Ibid.*, 489.

30 *The Will To Power* (written 1883-1888, first edition 1901), new edition revised and translated by Walter Kaufmann and R.J. Hollingdale, New York, Vintage Books, 1968, No,200, p.117.

between the two competing moralities of noble and slave could only have one outcome: the victory of the healthy man over the sick, wherein 'the bird of prey' always devours 'the tender lamb'.[31] But this is not now the case. For it is the extraordinary and wholly lamentable achievement of religion, and in particular of the priestly caste come to power in Judaism and Christianity, that it should channel its fear and loathing of its natural masters – of all that is brightest and best – into the creation of morality. Religious morality, in other terms, is *ressentiment* made flesh, binding the strong man with the cords of 'Thou shalt not', with a whole raft of life-denying commands, infecting the healthy mind with 'bad conscience' (*schlechtes Gewissen*): that, for example, sex is sinful, that the body is sinful, that every thought and action is sinful. Furthermore, and with a final twist of the knife, religion introduces the refinement of 'bad conscience': not merely bad conscience in relation to others but bad conscience in relation to God – a conscience, therefore, that can never find pardon because, whatever one does in mitigation, one remains forever guilty.

> In this spiritual cruelty there is a kind of insanity of the will which simply has no equal: a man's *will* finding him so guilty and reprehensible that there is no atonement, his *will* to imagine himself punished, but in such a way that the punishment could never be adequate for his crime, his *will* to infect and poison the most fundamental basis of things with the problem of punishment and guilt in order to cut himself off once and for all from any exit out of this labyrinth of 'fixed ideas', his *will* to erect an ideal – that of the 'holy God' – in order to be tangibly certain of his own absolute worthlessness when confronted with it. O this insane, sad beast man! What ideas it has, what unnaturalness, what paroxysms of nonsense, *what bestiality of thought* breaks from it as soon as it is prevented, if only a little, from being *a beast in deed*. . . . Here we have *illness* – no doubt about that – the most terrifying illness that has raged in human beings up to now: – and anyone who can still hear (but nowadays people no longer have the ear for that!) how in this night of torment and insanity the cry of *love* has resounded, the cry of the most yearning delight, of redemption through *love*, turns away, seized by an invincible horror. . . . In human beings there is so much that is terrible! . . . The world has already been a lunatic asylum for too long![32]

This in outline completes the first and critical part of Nietzsche's programme; and it leaves us with this crucial insight into the nature of

---

31 *The Genealogy of Morals*, translated by Ian Johnston.
32 *Ibid.*

morality. Morality in general, and Christian morality in particular, are not what they seem, i.e., the outcome of an absolute moral law or the conscious embodiment of the ultimate values prescribed by an infallibly just God; rather, they are the products of a deceit or subterfuge, camouflaging an ulterior motive, but one which Nietzsche's genealogical survey has now unmasked. *This hidden purpose is the defeat of the strong by the weak.* Take, for example, the Beatitudes of the Sermon on the Mount, so often regarded as a summation of Christian virtues. Here are paraded the poor and meek, those who turn the other cheek but who will yet inherit the Kingdom of God. This is the precise expression of 'herd morality', of a preference for disease rather than health, which, forged by the *ressentiment* of the slave towards his master, now ruthlessly brands in the pieties of religion all the natural life-affirming instincts of men as shameful 'sins' or 'guilts', as impulses and desires for which forgiveness must be asked in a life to come. This is the morality of the 'tarantulas', which fills the whole world with the storms of their revenge: "We shall wreak vengeance and abuse on all whose equals we are not" – thus do the tarantulas vow."[33]

The perception, however, that there exists a fundamental inequality between human beings – a perception recognized here by the priests but which only serves to fuel their jealousy and desire for revenge – now provides Nietzsche with the prologue to the second, and positive, phase of his programme. To reveal the truth that there is a fundamental *inequality* between human beings simultaneously unmasks the religious proposition – that all men are equal in the sight of God – as a metaphysical postulate of morality that is self-evidently untenable, as a verifiable inversion of the fact that there are some individuals who are not simply different from others but clearly superior. A universal code of ethics would perhaps be sustainable if moral agents were relevantly similar, but because agents are relevantly different, an all-embracing morality must necessarily do harm to some. What is thus required is a morality for these happy few. Here, then, the choice is between the prefabricated ethics of the domesticated herd animal, who cannot live his life without the fiction *that God lives*, and the morality 'beyond good and evil' of those exceptional sovereign and autonomous individuals of strength, to whom the secret has been revealed *that God is dead*. This truth, which the madman illuminated with his lantern, is the single most exhilarating fact of an atheistic culture: one is now liberated from the straitjacket of religion and the moralities of custom; but it also presents atheism with its most daunting challenge. The template of morality which God provided *external to life* must now be replaced by a morality *internal to life*. The death of God does not, that is to say, dissolve morality into a nihilistic acceptance that nothing is true

---

33 *Thus Spoke Zarathustra*, p.212.

and that life is valueless: it rather relocates the meaning of life *within life*, or rather and more particularly, within the individual who embraces life and rejects the ascetic ideal. The burden of morality, of defining what right conduct is, is thus removed from God and placed upon the shoulders of men, upon those who can bear the loneliness of living within a meaningless world *because one organizes a small portion of it oneself*[34] It is in this respect that the *Übermensch* is not man's successor but God's. For following God's obituary, this 'new man' must take on the God-like role of being the originator of truth and the creator of one's own moral self. The *Übermensch* accordingly designates a new kind of man, a *self-creating* individual, who is mankind's own supreme achievement, and totally different from the selfless and unegoistic individual lauded by Christianity.

The individual stands here as one of those 'free spirits of the first rank' who, as a kind of artist, freely shapes his own self as a work of art. This same idea is incorporated within the dominant conception of Nietzsche's later thought: the Will to Power (*Der Wille zur Macht*). Although often, and incorrectly, construed as the desire for power over others – an interpretation along racist lines which would legitimate the repressive and barbaric treatment of *untermenschen* and which Nietzsche would deplore as an example of the 'demon of power' – the Will to Power has more to do with self-sufficiency and self-confidence, with the self's own drive to foster its creative abilities in a world without dogmatic beliefs. The Will to Power, we should say, is the primary quality of the man of *moral action*, who, in his sheer zest for life, determines his own goals and who, unlike his passive and slavish counterpart, displays obedience not to the imposed norms of religion or society but only to *himself*. Thus the death of God, far from leading to the disintegration of one's self, now issues in a surge of optimism, in a liberation of all those natural instincts of life, to a resounding affirmation of life which was previously repressed by the guilt-inducing ordinances of God.[35]

There is one important amendment to make. If the world of formulaic religious morality is rapidly disappearing, it has not gone entirely, and indeed it remains for many people the consolation of their lives. Nietzsche is well aware of the seductive quality of religion: it offers answers to the perennial questions of what life is for, of why we should live in a particular way, of

---

34 *The Will to Power*, No.585 (A), p.318

35 Nietzsche's affirmation of life finds additional support in his doctrine of Eternal Recurrence, which I can only sketch here. The idea is that everything moves in an infinitely repeated circular course – a fact that should be enough to depress anyone. But this is not the case with the *Übermensch*. For such is his passionate affirmation of life that he embraces every moment of living even though knowing that all will be endlessly repeated. Once again utter futility is overcome by the indomitable will to power.

why pain exists, and it alleviates our anguish before death. To those secure in the comforts of religion, the *Übermensch* ideal will therefore remain a repugnant vision, offering none of these consolations. But the fact is that this security has been forever undermined by the death of God and that we now live in a post-theistic world. All else is illusory. Accordingly the comforts of moral certainty and final justification are already in the process of being replaced. So much we have seen already. And at first glance Nietzsche's replacement – his vision of the man who is a meaningful world unto himself – appears to be no more than an elitist individualist, who would doubtless endorse the Dostoevskian formula, with which I began this chapter, that 'If God is dead, then everything is permitted'. But things are not quite as they appear. For Nietzsche, the appearance of a higher form of humanity is not an end in itself but provides a model directing our aspirations, projecting us beyond what we are to what we might become. The *Übermensch* thus has wide *social* and *educative* implications, in the sense that he remains a *goal* which all should seek and some may attain, provided only that they live in an environment conducive to the exercise of their will to power and thus to their own individual flourishing. This is what Zarathustra means when he proclaims that the *Übermensch* is the 'meaning of the earth'.[36] The quest to become the autonomous author of one's own self is the only alternative left after God's death; and the very fact that Nietzsche provides no precise description of what this may entail – no exact recipe for moral conduct – only serves to highlight the enormous range of flourishing that is possible within the variety of individual efforts.

It is in this light that Nietzsche's position within the pantheon of atheists should be appreciated. Nietzsche is not an atheist in the comparatively straightforward mould of a Hume or a Russell, or in our own day of a Dawkins or a Dennett,[37] seeking to undermine belief by demolition, by showing the intellectual weakness of arguments for belief. Indeed, Nietzsche is frankly fairly dismissive of this approach: one proof only gives way to another, and, besides, since no proof ever caused faith, no counter-proof will ever demolish it. But more importantly, atheists of this stripe do not 'know how to make a clean sweep'.[38] In making this attempt Nietzsche stands as the prophet of a new post-metaphysical world, in which the meaning lost by the loss of God has been regained by a meaning found within the human range of self-discovery. This is a life-

---

36 *Thus Spoke Zarathustra*, p.125

37 Perhaps it is not surprising, then, that neither Dawkin's *The God Delusion* nor Hitchen's *God is not Great* (2007) makes any mention of Nietzsche, and that he appears in a solitary footnote in Sam Harris' *The End of Faith* (2004)

38 *The Daybreak*, translated by R.J. Hollingdale, with an introduction by Michael Tanner, Cambridge, Cambridge University Press, 1982, p. 93.

affirming philosophy meant to incite revolution within the realm of moral conduct by arousing our thirst for self-hood at that precise moment – at the 'twilight of the idols' – when the religious alternative has lost all value.

This type of atheism has sometimes been called 'axiological' or 'constructive' atheism, in as much as it offers a narrative of salvation – or more precisely a narrative of salvation *away from* salvation – which cannot proceed until the individual is first released from the gospel of a life-denying and death-obsessed religion, and comes to recognize, once and for all, that the world is without purpose or goal. Nietzsche's influence in this regard has been immense and is not just confined to philosophy. Nietzschean ideas are to be found in the psychology of Sigmund Freud and Alfred Adler, in the novels of Thomas Mann and Joseph Conrad, in the plays of Bernard Shaw, and in the poetry of Stefan George, Rainer Maria Rilke and W.B. Yeats. Understandably the philosophical line of influence is much easier to trace. Nietzsche is the immediate and acknowledged forerunner of what has come to be called *atheistic existentialism*. I am thinking here particularly of Martin Heidegger (1889-1976), Jean-Paul Sartre (1905-1980), Maurice Merleau-Ponty (1908-1961) and Albert Camus (1913-1960). Nor should one forget the so-called 'death of God' movement during the 1960s (whose membership included Paul van Buren, Thomas Altizer and William Hamilton), or the debt acknowledged to Nietzsche by George Betailles (1897-1962), Michel Foucault (1926-1984) and, much more recently, by Michel Onfray (b.1959), whose extraordinary polemic *In Defence of Atheism* (2007) is set specifically within a Nietzschean frame of reference.

All these philosophies have common Nietzschean themes. They are adamant that man is the exclusive measure of meaning and being, and that his baptism as the image of God is a morally reprehensible deception. They affirm that the powers of a human being are intrinsically part of him, and that it is this belief that gives dignity to his life, that radicalizes his ambition to improve his earthly lot and enhance the welfare of others, an ambition that would otherwise be mired in the fantasy of a life to come. While the atheistic way is the vehicle of what the existentialists call 'authenticity', and is marked by maturity, realism and creative power, the theistic way is marked by 'inauthenticity', by infantilism, delusion and abject submission, wherein one cravenly cedes to God the creative power that properly belongs to men alone. The religious ideal thus stands as the polar opposite of what Albert Camus has called 'the only original rule of life today: to learn to live and to die, and in order to be a man, to refuse to be a god'.[39]

---

39 *The Rebel*, Harmondsworth, Penguin Books, 1973, p.269.

6
Miracles

i. The Meaning of 'Miracle'

The term 'miracle' (Latin *miraculum*, from *mirari*: to wonder) designates an event (or person) of a particular and most peculiar kind: one that we may regard at the very least as something (or somebody) unusual, extraordinary or contrary to all our expectations. Thus it is that we speak of miraculous escapes, miraculous footballers, miraculous recoveries, miraculous skin creams and so on. For the believer, however, 'miracle' has a much more specific meaning. It refers to an occurrence so astounding that only God as its agent can explain it. Here a miracle stands as an external evidence of divine revelation, as an irruption into the natural order of things that would otherwise appear irrational or inexplicable without reference to the handiwork of God. In the New Testament the most common word for miracle is the Greek *semeion*, meaning 'sign'. This makes the matter clearer. A miracle is a sign by which God makes himself known within his own creation. In a demonstration of supernatural power, which astounds us by seeming to contradict the laws of nature and which accordingly provokes feelings of awe and amazement, God gives to certain witnesses a degree of perceptual confirmation of his existence not encountered anywhere else.

All the major religions have their miracles, and many of their principal personalities (e.g., Moses, Mohammad, Buddha) have their holy status confirmed by their ability to perform such mighty works. In Christianity, however, we find a particular commitment to the miraculous. The Gospels are replete with stories in which Jesus of Nazareth violates a law of nature: water changes into wine, the lame walk, the blind see, the deaf hear, lepers are cleansed, and the dead are returned to life. All these miracles attest to Jesus' divine nature, of his access to a supernatural power which confirms him as the Messiah (the 'anointed one'); but the supreme miracle to which the Church has pointed since its earliest days remains the miracle of Jesus' own resurrection from the dead. The disciples' conviction that this event had actually occurred is the historical starting-point of Christianity, without which, as Paul the Apostle makes clear, there would be no new religion to proclaim: 'If Christ has not been raised, then our preaching is in vain and your faith is in vain' (I *Corinthians* 15, vv.14-15).

Padre Pio

But if it should be supposed that miracles are only things of the biblical past, then we should look to the testimony and authentication of such events by the Christian communities since the death of Jesus. The great historian, Edward Gibbon, records that 'The Christian Church, from the time of the Apostles and their disciples, has claimed an uninterrupted succession of miraculous powers, the gift of tongues, of visions, and of prophecy, the power of expelling demons, of healing the sick and of raising the dead'.[1] Whole industries have grown up around the miracles associated with the bones of martyrs and the relics of saints, miracles of bodily preservation and miracles following the ecstatic vision of the Virgin Mary. Even today the lengthy process of canonization, in use since the tenth century, requires at least two attested miracles before any candidate can be proclaimed a saint. When one recalls that Pope John Paul II (1920-2005), who is himself being fast-tracked to sainthood, created more saints (482) than the combined total since 1588, then the number of miracles duly recorded and verified by the Vatican becomes truly prodigious.

Perhaps the most famous of Pope John Paul's saints is the Capuchin monk Padre Pio (born Francesco Forgione, 1887-1968), canonized in 2002. Venerated throughout Italy, and in popularity second only to Francis of Assisi, Padre Pio, like Francis before him, was said to have the stigmata, which duplicates on his body the five wounds of Christ on the Cross. Additionally, he was credited with a variety of miracles, with the powers of bilocation (of appearing in two different places simultaneously) and of levitation, of supernatural knowledge, and of exuding the 'odour of sanctity'. It has to be said that examination of his corpse in 1968 revealed no bodily wounds – although this was taken by some to be a miracle in itself – nor were any found at his exhumation forty years later, when the body went on display for several months in his home monastery of San Giovanni Rotondo. His shrine in the crypt receives seven-million pilgrims each year, and is second only in popularity

1 *TAC*: 274

to the Basilica of Guadalupe in Mexico City. This houses the miraculous image of the Virgin said to have appeared spontaneously in 1531 on the cloak of a peasant, Juan Diego, and subsequently another of Pope John Paul's successful candidates for sainthood, being canonized in the same year as Padre Pio.

Another equally famous divine portrait is the Shroud of Turin, a linen cloth measuring 4.6x1.1 meters, presently housed in the reliquary beneath the high altar in the Royal Chapel of the Cathedral of St. John the Baptist in Turin, Italy.

Detail on the Shroud of Turin

Because it bears the front and back imprints of an apparently crucified man, the cloth is supposedly the actual burial shroud of Jesus, and by the mid fourteenth century pilgrims, convinced of its miraculous powers, were flocking to see it in the little church at Lirey in north central France, where it was first kept. In 1578 the Shroud was moved to Turin, and in 1898 the town council commissioned Seconda Pia to photograph it. To Pia's astonishment, he discovered that the negative revealed a much more lifelike image of the figure than could be detected with the naked eye, and one which, moreover, detailed injuries to wrists, feet and back. These findings were sufficient to convince Pia that he was face-to-face with an image of the crucified Christ and before long the Cathedral was besieged by crowds, equally certain of the Shroud's miraculous provenance. The Vatican, however, fearing a hoax, was much more cautious and investigations were initiated. These were by and large inconclusive; but in 1988, in a surprise move, the Vatican allowed the shroud to be carbon dated by three independent sources – by Oxford University, the University of Arizona, and the Swiss Federal Institute of Technology in Zurich. These concluded that the cloth was medieval, dating somewhere between 1260-1390, thus supporting the conclusion that the image was a fake. This has not deterred shroudologists. The cloth was apparently in a fire during the early part of the sixteenth century and it is this which is said to account for the erroneous dating.

One other important set of miracles is worth mentioning. These are the miracles of healing recorded at Lourdes, a French town at the foot of the Pyrenees. In 1858 in the grotto of Massabielle by the river Gave, the Virgin Mary, later identifying herself as 'The Immaculate Conception', appeared eighteen times to Bernadette Soubirous, a fourteen-year-old peasant girl. On the ninth visit, she told Bernadette to drink from the spring and wash in the water. With no spring visible, the girl began to scratch in the gravel. A bubbling pool rose up which, by the following day, had become a full stream. In two other visitations, the Lady asked Bernadette to build a chapel at the grotto site and to have the faithful come in processions to it. On the fifteenth visitation, 20,000 people jammed Lourdes, and soldiers were brought in to control the crowds. Unsurprisingly there was some initial scepticism, and many of the earliest investigators, including the local priest Abbé Dominique Peyramale, were convinced they were dealing with a hoax. Although Peyramale later changed his mind, it took four years of further investigation before the Church approved devotion to Our Lady of Lourdes. As for Bernadette herself, she later joined the convent of the Sisters of Charity at Nevers, dying there at the early age of thirty-five in 1879. Her body was exhumed three times and said to be 'incorrupt' – i.e., preserved from decomposition – a miracle which supported her own canonization in 1933.

Lourdes today is a phenomenon, boasting, it is said, more tourist rooms and hotel beds than anywhere in France, except Paris. A basilica was built above the grotto in 1876, and a vast underground church was added in 1958, with seating for 25,000 worshippers. But what of the miracles? What makes them particularly interesting is that they are so well documented. In 1883 the Lourdes Medical Bureau was set up to investigate cases, to establish whether a particular cure was 'medically inexplicable'; but it was not the duty of the Bureau to decide whether a miracle had occurred – that remained the prerogative of the Church. The strike-rate has not been impressive. Since its foundation the Bureau has examined the records of more than 7,000 people claiming that they were cured after visiting the sanctuaries, and of these only 67 have been pronounced miracles. Statistics further suggest that, as access to professional medical care has increased, so the number of recorded miracles has decreased. The Bureau recorded 5000 inexplicable cases before 1947, at a rate of 78 per year; but the rate dropped dramatically from 1947 to 1980 to less than one per year. It should be said, however, that even these findings have been considered suspect by other medical specialists, who point out, not unreasonably, that what is considered incurable now may not be in the future, and that, more often than not, the recoveries cited do not relate to organ replacement or regeneration (e.g., the regrowth of a severed hand)

Bernadette Soubirous

but to diseases that could well have psychosomatic origin (e.g., Parkinson's disease) or in which spontaneous regression is not unknown (e.g., multiple sclerosis). It was miracles such as these that prompted the French author Anatole France (1844-1924), on seeing the discarded canes and crutches at the grotto, to remark, 'What, no wooden legs?' Small wonder, then, that even the doctors at the Bureau have become increasingly wary of pronouncing on such cases, and that in 2008 they officially distanced themselves from the Church's pronouncements on miracles, conceding that they were no longer competent to judge on such matters.[2]

In all these cases a miracle is understood as a violation of a law of nature; and it is not difficult to call up further examples, such as weeping icons, bleeding effigies, moving statues, and the quite dazzling array of wonders worked by relics associated with Jesus: by pieces of the true cross, by the crown of thorns, by hay from the manger, by his baby hair, and by his foreskin preserved in no less than six churches. Miracles like these have been exhaustively detailed by Joe Nickell in his *Looking for a Miracle* (1993), and his findings are enough to dent the beliefs of all but the most ardent papal enthusiasts.[3] If we then couple Nickell's work with that of James Randi, a plausible account emerges of why such things could even begin to be believed. Randi is today the foremost investigator and demystifier of paranormal and pseudoscientific claims: it was he who exposed 'psychic' spoon-benders and the fraudulent tricks of faith-healers, such as the American evangelist, the Reverend Peter Popoff.[4]

2 *International Herald Tribune*, 3 December, 2008.
3 Prometheus Books, Amherst, New York, 1993.
4 See Randi's *The Truth about Uri Geller*, Prometheus Books, Buffalo, New York, 1982; *Flim-Flam! – The Truth about Unicorns, Parapsychology and Other Delusions*, New York, Harper & Row, 1980; *The Faith Healers*, Prometheus Books, Buffalo, New York, 1989; and *An Encyclopedia of Claims, Frauds, and Hoaxes of the Occult and Supernatural*, New York, St Martin's Press, 1995. Many of Randi's exposés can be watched on *www.youtube.com*.

If we take Randi's evidence at face value, and as his own 'miraculous' demonstrations seem to suggest, many miracles would then appear to be the result of frauds perpetrated upon the credulous by hoaxers and religious imposters; and that a clever magician, like Randi, can make one believe that what is happening quite naturally is something else, i.e., evidence of supernatural intervention. This is not to say that all miracles are hoaxes; but it does at least raise the possibility that, when set within highly-charged situations such as these, an event contravening natural law never occurred, even though witnesses may

Friedrich Schleiermacher

attest to it occurring, and that saying that it has occurred remains part of a story told by those inclined to believe from the outset that such improbable things do actually happen.

These are considerations which we shall have to explore further. For the moment, however, it is worth noting that it is not only atheists who regard miracles as intellectually embarrassing. For many believers as well the idea is hard to stomach and one that they regard as an affront to the rational mind. According to the leading twentieth-century theologian, Paul Tillich (1886-1965), the notion that a miracle is a violation of natural law leads directly to 'irrationalist rationalism', in which 'the degree of absurdity in a miracle story becomes the measure of its religious value. The more impossible, the more revelatory!'[5] Many distinguished theologians have agreed with Tillich; and in his own *Perspectives on Nineteenth and Twentieth Century Protestant Thought* (1967), he cites many authors who, reflecting the anti-supernatural and positivistic bias of the period, precluded from the outset any notion of the miraculous.[6] His list reads like a roll-call of the great and the good of European, and almost exclusively German, theology. The most prominent is Friedrich Schleiermacher (1768-1834), who, in his *The Christian Faith* (1821-1882), proposes a naturalistic critique of miracles. Because God ordains and presides over a closed 'system of nature', one that is entirely governed by the universal laws of natural causation, no room is left for any possible suspension. So, if we are to call anything a miracle, it is because it is perceived as such,

5 *Systematic Theology*, Volume 1, London, James Nisbetm 1953, p.128
6 ed. C.E. Braaten, New York, Harper and Row, 1967.

Ernst Troeltsch

because it transmits to the witness feelings of religious awe, thereby stimulating 'the pious consciousness', but not because anything has (or could) actually happen.[7]

But if miracle, in the sense of supernatural intervention, was for Schleiermacher irreconcilable with our scientific notions of causation, it was for other theologians equally objectionable on grounds of historical method. For Ernst Troeltsch (1865-1923) the historian must operate according to the principle of 'analogy', by which he meant that judgments about whether something did or did not occur in the past must be made on the basis of whether such things do or do not occur in the present: an analogy, in other words, is assumed between past and present. This point he clarifies in an important early essay (1898): 'Agreement with normal, customary, or at least frequently attested happenings and conditions as we have experienced them is the criterion of probability for all events that historical criticism can recognize as having actually or possibly happened'.[8] This was enough for Troeltsch to reject the possibility of miracles. For by agreeing that people do not rise bodily from the dead in our present world and experience, we can leave no basis for assuming that any individual could have done so in the past.

Such naturalistic assumptions, at work in all these authors, are also to be found in a third group, for which miracles were objectionable not so much on scientific or historical grounds but on theological. Miracles should be discarded because any belief in supernatural intervention betrays an outdated *mythological* outlook which expects God to reveal himself by such extraordinary means. The classic representative of this view is D.F. Strauss (1808-1874), whose *Das Leben Jesus* of 1835, translated into English by George Eliot, caused a sensation, and effectively ruined

---

7   *The Christian Faith*, translated by H.R. Mackintosh and J.S. Stuart, London, T. & T. Clark, 1999, pp.71-73.

8   'Historical and Dogmatic Method in Theology' (1898) in *Religion in History*, trans. James Luther Adams and Walter F. Bense, Minneapolis, Fortress Press, 1991, pp.13-14.

Strauss' chances of ever obtaining a university position. If, previous to Strauss, the application of myth had been confined to the stories of Jesus' entrance into and departure from the world, Strauss now included all the stories prior to the baptism, the baptism itself, the mission of the seventy, the miracles of 'healing' and 'nature', the transfiguration and the resurrection. None of these stories, he held, can be properly regarded as

D.F. Strauss

historical for in them all the mythopoetic process is at work: rather, they are the creation of mythologically-minded authors, who, ignorant of the universal laws of nature, were totally at home in a world very different from our own and peopled by spirits, demons, and wonder-workers. Strauss, accordingly, offers this criterion to distinguish the historical from the unhistorical in the gospels:

> First. When the narration is irreconcilable with the known and universal laws which govern the course of events. . . .When therefore we meet with an account of certain phenomena or events of which it is either expressly stated or implied that they were produced by God himself (divine apparitions, voices from heaven and the like), or by human beings possessed of supernatural powers (miracles, prophecies), such an account is in so far to be considered as not historical.[9]

The school that followed Strauss – the so-called 'liberal Protestants', among whom were Albrecht Ritschl (1822-1889) and Adolf von Harnack (1851-1930) – were to develop this scepticism about miracles still further; but the high point for the school was undoubtedly reached with Rudolf Bultmann (1884-1976). Bultmann similarly upholds a view of history as a closed continuum of events, and wholeheartedly applies Troeltsch's principal of analogy to exclude any supernatural interventions

9   *The Life of Jesus Critically Examined* (1835), translated from the 4th German edition by George Eliot, London, Chapman Brothers, 1846, p.71.

Rudolf Bultmann

in history. So, in his influential article 'New Testament and Mythology' of 1941, he remarks that our scientific and technological control of the world have developed to such a degree that we can no longer believe in the spirit and wonder world of the gospels, and that such a modern attitude makes, for example, the belief that a dead man could be resuscitated (i.e., the miracle of the Resurrection) quite impossible.[10] Later, in a series of lectures delivered in the United States in 1951 Bultmann made his position even clearer:

The whole conception of the world which is presupposed in the preaching of Jesus as in the New Testament generally is mythological; i.e., the conception of the world as being structured in three stories, heaven, earth, and hell; the conception of the intervention of supernatural powers in the course of event; and the conception of miracles, especially the conception of the intervention of supernatural powers in the inner life of the soul, the conception that men can be tempted and corrupted by the devil and possessed by evil spirits.[11]

We can see from this the extent to which Bultmann's radical programme of 'demythologization' was, like that of his predecessors, steeped in the epistemological certainty that 'the cause-and-effect nexus' was absolute, and that accordingly miracles, if thought of as disruptions of natural processes, must be *a priori* excluded from any modern appreciation of how the world turns. This certainly tempers the view that miracles are no more than frauds perpetrated upon the credulous. A great gulf, of many centuries, is fixed between the belief in miracles and the present-day rejection of them; and any contemporary belief that such things may still occur must to some

---

10 Available in *Kerygma and Myth*, Volume 1, edited by H.W. Bartsch and translated by R.H. Fuller, London, SPCK, 1964, pp.1-44.
11 *Jesus Christ and Mythology*, New York, Charles Scribner's Sons, 1958, p.15.

extent be intellectually irresponsible, having succumbed to, or been culturally conditioned by, the outmoded and entirely fanciful categories of a world-view no longer viable.

From this brief and simplified sketch, it would seem that, with so many distinguished theologians on their side, atheists need not bother overmuch about miracles. But this is not the case. There is yet another definition of miracles, to which both Tillich and Schleiermacher subscribe, one which, while certainly jettisoning altogether the notion of violation, can yet designate the occurrence as an act of God. This we may call the *contingency definition of the miraculous*. Contingency miracles are extremely rare coincidences, which, when set within a religious framework, have religious significance. As coincidences these events occur quite naturally and are thus capable of natural explanation; but for those who witness them they remain revelations of God. The philosopher R.F. Holland has given a well-known example of what is meant.[12] Suppose that a young boy gets stuck on a railway line near his house; and suppose further that an express train is coming towards him. The child's mother screams at her son, but to no avail. But the train stops short of the child, and the mother thanks God for the miracle. But it is no miracle. The brakes were automatically applied because the driver had fainted; and he had fainted because of high blood pressure induced by an exceptionally heavy lunch and a quarrel with a colleague.

The important point to notice in Holland's story is that the mother continues to believe that what she witnessed was a miracle, and this despite the fact that she accepts the natural explanation of why the train stopped. What makes this event a miracle for her is not, then, that the course of nature has been disrupted in any way but rather that she attributes a particular meaning to an event that a non-believer would attribute to coincidence. Thus, concludes Holland, to call an event miraculous is to view it as a religiously significant event, as an event whose truth or falsehood cannot be settled solely by an analysis of the available evidence, because what will count as evidence cannot be isolated from the perspective of the believer.

The trouble with the contingency definition of miracle is not hard to see. Both the believer and the non-believer may witness the same event; but the believer attributes a meaning to the event, while the non-believer does not. There is accordingly no *public* evidence of a miracle occurring, since, indeed, the only evidence that is required is the believer's subjective conviction that something extraordinary has occurred. All that is

---

12 'The Miraculous', *American Philosophical Quarterly*, 2, 1965, pp.43-44. Reprinted in my *The Philosophy of Religion*, Volume I, Cambridge, The Lutterworth Press, 2008, pp.271-273. Hereafter cited as *PR*.

sufficient, in other words, for the son's escape to be called a miracle is for the mother to see it as such. But this is very weak. For it is simply not the case that a statement is true because someone is convinced that it is. Take the proposition 'The mother is certain that event X is a miracle'. This may be true in so far as it tells us something about the psychological state of the mother in relation to X: that X was special for her, that it changed her life, and so on. But the truth of the assertion that this was indeed how the mother felt about X does not entail that she was correct in her judgment about X, that it was indeed a revelation of God, who had in this special event intervened to save her son. In this respect, therefore, subjective certainty cannot be the measure of historical truth; and that I might experience a particular sensation through the medium of an event – even affirming that 'I thank God for saving my son's life'– does not of itself justify the conclusion that there exists something distinct from that sensation as its cause, and which I may thus discount as a fiction. This does not, of course, rule out the possibility that what the mother saw *really was a miracle*, that it was indeed a divine revelation of some sort. But in that case, we need some criterion by which to judge between experiences, between the experience that says something has occurred and the experience that says nothing has occurred. For if it isn't publicly and empirically evident that X is a miracle, then we must suppose that there is something unique in the *experience of X* itself that allows us to say that this event, and not another, is a miracle and thus a sign of God's presence. But no criterion is forthcoming and thus we get nowhere. All that we end up with is a description of a psychological state, from which no conclusions can be drawn other than that the believer believes that she is not delusional and that what she has seen is a real revelation. But deluded she may be.

The fairly obvious weaknesses of the notion of contingency miracles returns us to the traditional view of miracles, held by a sufficiently large number of believers to make it still troublesome for atheists. For while atheists have no problem with an event which has already been classified as continuous with nature, and whose only special claim to fame derives from the particular psychological, and, they would argue, almost certainly deluded disposition of its witness, they have much more trouble with violation-miracles, with the emphatic assertion by believers that God has decisively intervened in history, and so broken the causal nexus. This is so for two main reasons. First, the atheist has to deal with the extensive *evidence of testimony*; that such things have not only actually happened but have been *seen* to happen. This testimony, despite the efforts of James Randi and others, can appear to be quite precise and confirmed by many who cannot so easily be diagnosed as suffering from the fantasies of the credulous. The second reason is this. The atheist is not merely up against the evidence of testimony but also, and uniquely so in Christianity, against the *necessity* that such evidence be true: that, in other words, the central statement of the Christian creed – that God was incarnate in the historical person of Jesus of Nazareth – be irrefutably endorsed by the miracles that he himself performed and, most especially, by the miracle of his resurrection, without which there would be no gospel to preach. This being the case, believers are quite entitled to employ Troeltsch's analogy for their own ends. For if miracles can be established to have happened in the present, there is no reason to suppose that they did not happen in the past. The miracle stories of the gospel history may thus vindicated by contemporary experience.

ii. The Critique of Miracles: Their Impossibility

The first thing to do is to consider the objection just given: that miracles, if defined as a violation of the laws of nature, constitute an infringement of a causal regularity, or a supernatural disruption of a 'closed system', and are thus quite impossible. Any claims, therefore, that miracles do occur or have occurred, and from whatever source, can be dismissed without further ado, no matter how strong the evidential support may be. This line of attack is not peculiar to atheists, and we have met it just now among theologians as well. One of the classic presentations of this argument is given by the Dutch-Jewish philosopher Baruch Spinoza (1632-1677); and we should note that Schleiermacher cites Spinoza as the major influence upon his own rejection of the violation-concept of the miraculous. Presented in Chapter Six of his *Tractatus Theologico-Politicus* (1670) Spinoza argues that, because nature keeps to a fixed and immutable order (*fixum et immuabilem ordinem*), nothing can occur in nature which contravenes her universal laws. Thus a miracle, which is such a contravention, 'is a mere absurdity'. 'We may, then', he continues, 'be absolutely certain that every event which is truly described in Scripture necessarily happened, like everything else, according to natural laws'.[13]

A modern update of Spinoza's argument has been provided by the contemporary philosopher, Alastair McKinnon.[14] For Mckinnon a miracle is an impossibility because 'the idea of a suspension of natural law is self-contradictory'. His reasoning is as follows. Given that natural laws

---

13 See *The Chief Works of Benedict de Spinoza*, translated with an Introduction by R.H.M. Elwes, London, Constable, 1951, pp.81-87. This translation is available at www.gutenberg.org. See also *TAC*: 266-272.

14 "'Miracle' and 'Paradox'", *American Philosophical Quarterly*, 4, 1967, pp.308-314. The article is reprinted in *PR*, 1: 243-245.

Baruch Spinoza

are 'simply highly generalized shorthand descriptions of how things do in fact happen' – they do no more than describe the actual course of events – any claim that particular suspension of a particular law has occurred must be in fact either a misreading of the law or an inadequate understanding of the law. Any assertion that miracles have happened is thereby rendered false by definition. For given that it is *a priori* true that laws of nature state what happens, anything that happens must conform to those laws. Thus anything that may initially appear to be a miracle, must in fact be something else, i.e., an instance of an amended law. If the believer refuses to do this, and continues to claim that X was indeed a violation of a natural law, then all he or she has done instead is to assert that the event lies outside the orbit of how things happen and so is not an event. So, to give an example: if Lazarus really did rise from the dead, this is not evidence of a miracle but evidence that our original ideas about bodily decomposition will have to be reassessed. If the believer continues to believe in Lazarus' resurrection, then he or she is believing in an event which by definition did not occur.

This argument figures prominently within the atheistic tradition, although admittedly rarely expressed as forcefully as this; and it stretches out beyond Spinoza to embrace all those who, however they may individually conceive of the workings of nature, nevertheless treat nature as a whole as a 'closed system', as a uniformity of cause and effect, one which cannot therefore be 'open' to any supernatural penetration; and the fact that many believers here agree with non-believers, so presenting a united front on the point, only serves to give this line of argument still greater prominence. It includes, therefore, Epicurus and Lucretius, and d'Holbach as well as Voltaire – the last-named spending a good deal of his time ridiculing miracles as a mixture of fraud and ignorance.[15] As a brief

---

15 See Voltaire's entry on 'Miracles' in his *Philosophical Dictionary*, and published by Penguin Books as *Miracles and Idolatry*, 2005. Voltaire is a great collector of miracles. My own favourite is the following: 'a certain monk was so much

footnote, it is worth repeating that Voltaire was no atheist – although he mistakenly regarded Spinoza as one – and that he is more usually classed as a deist.[16] Deism, though short-lived as a movement, was particularly conspicuous among the philosophes of mid eighteenth-century France, was popular in England in the last years of the seventeenth and the first half of the eighteenth century, and is represented in the United States by an illustrious group: John Quincy Adams (1767-1848), Benjamin Franklin (1706-1790), Thomas Jefferson (1743-1826), George Washington (1732-1799) and Thomas Paine (1737-1809), whose *The Age of Reason* (1794) is perhaps the most famous of all deist treatises, with a clear line of descent back to Spinoza.

> Of all the modes of evidence that ever were invented to obtain belief to any system or opinion to which the name of religion has been given, that of miracle, however successful the imposition may have been, is the most inconsistent. For, in the first place, whenever recourse is had to show, for the purpose of procuring that belief (for a miracle, under any idea of the word, is a show) it implies a lameness or weakness in the doctrine that is preached. And, in the second place, it is degrading the Almighty into the character of a show-man, playing tricks to amuse and make the people stare and wonder. It is also the most equivocal sort of evidence that can be set up; for the belief is not to depend upon the thing called a miracle, but upon the credit of the reporter, who says that he saw it; and, therefore, the thing, were it true, would have no better chance of being believed than if it were a lie.
>
> Suppose I were to say, that when I sat down to write this book, a hand presented itself in the air, took up the pen and wrote every word that is herein written; would any body believe me? Certainly they would not. Would they believe me a whit the

---

in the habit of performing miracles, that the prior at length forbade him to exercise his talent in that line. The monk obeyed; but seeing a poor tiler fall from the top of a house, he hesitated for a moment between the desire to save the unfortunate man's life, and the sacred duty of obedience to his superior. He merely ordered the tiler to stay in the air till he should receive further instructions, and ran as fast as his legs would carry him to communicate the urgency of the circumstances to the prior. The prior absolved him from the sin he had committed in beginning the miracle without permission, and gave him leave to finish it, provided he stopped with the same, and never again repeated his fault'. Voltaire concludes that 'philosophers may certainly be excused for entertaining a little doubt of this legend'. This text is also available at http://libertyfund.org/

16 See above, pp.42-43

Thomas Paine

more if the thing had been a fact? Certainly they would not. Since then a real miracle, were it to happen, would be subject to the same fate as the falsehood, the inconsistency becomes the greater of supposing the Almighty would make use of means that would not answer the purpose for which they were intended, even if they were real.[17]

Although differing widely in certain matters of belief – for example, on the question of the immortality of the soul and whether or not rewards and punishments are to be expected in the after-life – the deists are sufficiently self-consistent to justify their collective title. Working out the implications of Newtonian physics, they adopted a view of God as the master of eternal matter, as the divine creator of a mechanistic universe, which, once created, moves according to its own immutable laws – laws that can be discovered through human reason and scientific enquiry – and which thus leaves no room for any supernatural intervention on God's part. It was not, then, through divine revelation that God is known; rather, nature itself is the fingerprint of God which human reason – itself a higher authority than revelation – observes and learns from, and from which it constructs all that is needed to lead a moral and religious life.

---

17 *The Age of Reason*, collected and edited by Moncure Daniel Conway, London, Routledge/Thoemmes Press, 1996. Available at www.gutenberg.org. See also *TAC*: 280-284

But let us return to the matter at hand, to the argument to which all these distinguished men subscribe, namely that miracles are by definition impossible. Given that it is an *a priori* truth that laws of nature state what happens, anything that happens must conform to those laws. Thus anything that may at first appear a violation must in principle be something else, that is, an instance of an amended law. Thus there can be no violations of the laws and so no miracles.

This argument, despite its distinguished pedigree, is, however, not nearly as strong as it appears. The definition that miracles are impossible stands upon the back of another definition, namely, that the laws which operate in the natural world are deterministic, that everything that occurs must operate within the arena of universal causation, that every event must have its cause. But this second definition, as David Hume has taught us, cannot be so easily sustained. Let us recall here Hume's criticism of the cosmological argument.[18] That every event has a cause is assumed to be the case not because it is either intuitively obvious or demonstrable but because there is a 'determination of the mind', a psychological disposition on our part, to make this assumption. To believe that A causes B, and that the connection between them is a necessary one, derives, in other words, from the experience of seeing them constantly conjoined, and it is this which generates in us the habit of expectation that this will always be the case. But this is not so. For while the notion of causality is undoubtedly central to our understanding of the world, it is not one that can be logically established but is one derived from our mistaken projection into the world of our belief that nature is uniform; that what has been the case remains the blueprint for what will always be the case. But, as Hume remarked, there is no valid logical justification for saying that 'instances, of which we have no experience, must resemble those, of which we have had experience, and that the course of nature continues always the same'.[19] So while we may expect the sun to rise tomorrow because it always has – and indeed order our lives upon that expectation – there is no guarantee that it will, since there is no self-evident or demonstrable reason why future experiences must conform to past experiences. This argument immediately undermines the claim that miracles, when regarded as violations of nature, are logically impossible. For to say that they are logically impossible is to make the assumption that the laws of nature are invariable and brook no exceptions, which is an assumption that cannot be sustained. We are left, then, with the (perhaps surprising) conclusion that miracles are logically legitimate, and that interventions into a 'closed' system of nature are possible.

---

18 See above, pp. 45-49

19 *A Treatise of Human Nature* (1739), Book 1, Section VI, ed. L.A. Selby-Bigge, London, Oxford University Press, reprint 1965, p.89. See above pp.45-49

David Hume

iii. The Critique of Miracles: Their Improbability

But the believer should not breathe a sigh of relief too quickly. For having established that miracles are possible, Hume now proceeds to his own dismissal of miracles as intrinsically improbable. This argument appears in the essay 'Of Miracles', which forms part of his *Enquiry Concerning Human Understanding* (1748). Hume rated this work very highly, claiming that it provided 'an everlasting check to all kinds of superstitious delusion, and consequently, will be useful as long as the world endures'.[20] In Hume's own lifetime it was his most famous and controversial piece of writing, and for positive atheists it remains the locus classicus of all subsequent debate on miracles.[21]

---

20 *Enquiries Concerning Human Understanding and Concerning the Principles of Morals*, ed. L. A. Selby-Bigge, 3rd edition with text revised and notes by P.H. Nidditch, Oxford, Clarendon Press, 1975, p.110.
21 See *TAC*: 285-295

Let us assume, for purposes of argument, that an event X has occurred and that all the witnesses have agreed that it did. If we are the judge, how do we assess their evidence? What we do first, says Hume, is determine whether they are trustworthy – whether, for example, they are generally honest or whether they have a vested interest in saying what they do; but having established they are to be trusted, we move on to the next stage, to a consideration of whether or not the event is intrinsically probable or improbable. Now we have to choose between two competing and equally justifiable positions: we have to decide whether the possibility of these (otherwise trustworthy) witnesses being deliberately misleading or being themselves mislead is greater that the possibility of the event X occurring. But how do we determine whether event X is improbable or not? This we do, continues Hume, by employing a fundamental principle of *inductive reasoning*, i.e., that the more I see A followed by B, the greater is my expectation that A will be followed by B in the future. I assume, that is, that *this* rubber ball will bounce because I have seen rubber balls so often bouncing *before*; and my belief that rubber balls bounce will increase or decrease proportionate to the amount of empirical evidence that supports their bouncing or not. This, then, is how we determine whether event X is intrinsically improbable or not: it is established on the evidence gathered about how things have invariably happened in the past, which also counts as evidence of the high likelihood of their future repetition. This explains why we can dismiss the claim that 'Max, who lives in Brighton, is over 200 years old'. He may well live in Brighton – that is something we can verify - but that he is as old as this is extremely improbable, given the ages of all those who have lived before him.

Turning now to miracles, the same inductive procedure is to be followed. Hume defines a miracle as 'a transgression of a law of nature by a particular volition of the Deity, or by the interposition of some invisible agent'.[22] So what is a law of nature? A law of nature, we may say, is a summary of an induction, that is, of an observed empirical invariance. So many As have been observed to be Bs – indeed no A has ever been observed not to be a B – that we may lay down the general principle, thereby elevating it to the status of a natural law, that 'All As are Bs'. Thus we may re-define a miracle not as an impossible event – following Hume's earlier remarks – but as an event which runs counter to all known experience, that is, experience as summarized in the law of nature. For this reason, to call anything a miracle is to admit to a proportionate lack of evidence. If the event X is to be counted a miracle, it must violate the evidence of innumerable past experiences that goes to make the law; and since all the accumulated empirical evidence relevant

22 *Ibid.*, p.115

to the law has confirmed it as having no exceptions, the evidence supporting the event being a violation must be discounted in favour of the evidence which says that no such violation occurred. So the story of the saint, who following his beheading, walked a few hundred yards to a cathedral with his head under his arm is dismissed not because it is *a priori* impossible but because it is *a posteriori* improbable: it runs counter to our common and invariable experience of the world. The weight of evidence always lies with those who deny the miracle. Thus if 'a wise man . . . proportions his belief to the evidence',[23] he must agree that denying that Jesus rose from the dead is always the reasonable thing to do, no matter how trustworthy the witnesses.

> There must, therefore, be a uniform experience against every miraculous event, otherwise the event would not merit that appellation. And as a uniform experience amounts to a proof, there is here a direct and full proof, from the nature of the fact, against the existence of any miracle; nor can such a proof be destroyed, or the miracle rendered credible, but by an opposite proof, which is superior.[24]

Hume is fond of employing court-room analogies, and it is worth elaborating one here. In the argument just advanced, the case brought against the likelihood of the miracle-event occurring is not so much that the witnesses are unreliable (although we may later discover that they are) but that there is a lack of *evidential support*: that against the evidence of such things occurring, the judge sets the much greater evidence, summarized in the natural law, that such things are extremely unlikely ever to occur. So no investigation on the judge's part is required to determine what happened: he need only refer to the rubric of invariability prescribed by the law. But since this Humean judge has already allowed that an exception is possible – that a miracle, although highly improbable, could occur – it is interesting to speculate on how a judicial investigation into this one unique instance might proceed.

Let us take a resurrection as our test case. The judge knows that such an event runs counter to the accumulated evidence of innumerable past instances, and that it is upon this evidence that the natural law is held to be contingently (if not necessarily) true. This law reads: 'No person, once dead, comes back to life'; and it is a law that we all accept, the bereaved and funeral directors alike. But in one unique case – say, the case of Lazarus – something quite exceptional is said to have occurred, and Lazarus, certainly once dead, revived. Now if we dismiss, for purposes

---

23 *Ibid.*, p.110.
24 *Ibid.*, p.115.

of argument, that this was not a case of fraud or mis-diagnosis, how is a judge to determine the truth of the matter? Here the philosopher Antony Flew introduces an important variant on Hume's argument.[25] The judge's position is now not dissimilar from that of an historian assessing evidence of whether something has happened in the past; and given that he does not himself possess direct knowledge of Lazarus' recovery – he was not there when it happened – he must proceed indirectly, and reconstruct the event on the basis of the evidence before him now, on evidence that the judge has immediate access to. And what the judge now knows is how the world now operates, namely, that it operates according to certain natural laws, which allow him to decide whether any event has higher or lower degrees of probability. This is not to say that the judge believes that no exceptions to the law are possible; it is rather – and this is the crucial point – that he accepts amendments of the law only when such alterations are subject to repeated verification. So the reason why a judge would still dismiss the Lazarus-case is not because he maintains that the case involves a logical impossibility but because the claim 'Dead people can come back to life' is contrary to his own first-hand knowledge of those regularities of the world which scientific knowledge has directly verified as empirically true. The only way, then, that this judge would accept that Lazarus did what is claimed he did would be to certify experimentally that others have done the same and repeatedly. But the repetition can hardly be said to establish the exception but only that the natural law should be amended.

This is a persuasive and important strengthening of Hume's case, and recalls Troeltsch's principle of analogy: that we are able to make judgments of probability about past events only on the assumption that what we experience now is not so very different from what others experienced then; and that it is a legitimate inference to suppose that what I now know about decapitation makes it highly implausible that (as has been alleged) any ancient martyrs spoke after their beheading. The same inference is at work when we say that the Old Testament probably got it right when it says that the whale swallowed Jonah, and not Jonah the whale, and probably got it wrong when it records that Joshua commanded the sun to stand still in the heavens. To repeat, nothing in Hume's (or Flew's) argument prohibits the logical possibility of such things occurring: not regarding laws of nature as analytic truths of logic, neither can establish that miracles cannot occur. But then this is not their primary concern anyway. The weight of their argument falls rather against the testimonial evidence for such events; and that the

---

25 Flew's argument was first presented in his *Hume's Philosophy of Belief*, London, Routledge & Kegan Paul, 1961, pp.186-187.

historian, when examining the relevant documents which reports such things, will, in the light of present knowledge, always conclude that they are so highly improbable as to be entirely discounted. The burden of proof thus lies with the believer to provide pertinent and additional evidence to demonstrate that, in these few cases, documents faithfully record a violation of a natural law – that Lazarus rose from the dead as reported – and that the scientific evidence marshalled against such an event happening does not in this specific instance apply. Thereafter the judge, if he be wise, can do no more than proportion his belief to the evidence before him.

This concludes the first part of Hume's essay on miracles. In the second, Hume turns away from his philosophical critique and considers more practical matters to do with the witnesses themselves. Having previously assumed, purely for the purposes of argument, that the witnesses of miracles are trustworthy, Hume now says that in actual fact they rarely are. Hume's claim here is by and large a rehearsal of the familiar one that the witnesses of miracles are generally speaking credulous and gossipy creatures of poor education, and we need not repeat them here. But Hume introduces one new argument of importance:

> . . . let us consider, that, in matters of religion, whatever is different is contrary; and that it is impossible the religions of ancient Rome, of Turkey, of Siam, and of China should, all of them, be established on any solid foundation. Every miracle, therefore, pretended to have been wrought in any of these religions (and all of them abound in miracles), as its direct scope is to establish the particular system, it likewise destroys the credit of those miracles, on which that system was established; so that all the prodigies of different religions are to be regarded as contrary facts; and the evidences of these prodigies, whether weak or strong, as opposite to each other.[26]

This is a novel argument and one which, I believe, carries considerable weight. The veracity of the witness-statements that a miracle has occurred is here challenged not because the witnesses are themselves held to be unreliable – even though that may be the case – but because their witness-statements are challenged by other witness-statements *in other religions*. The New Testament records that Jesus performed miracles; and the Islamic tradition does the same for the prophet Mohammad, his reception of the divine Qur'an from the angel Gabriel being the principal example. The Old Testament similarly details the fact that Moses performed miracles, at one point winning a miracle competition

---

26 *Ibid.*, pp.121-122.

with Egyptian sorcerers, who, incidentally, could also perform them but who were let down when it came to the gnats (*Exodus* 8, v.16); and Buddhist commentaries describe at great length the miracles of Siddhartha Gautama, who in one famous burst of energy demonstrated his extraordinary powers over a period of fifteen days. All these miracles stand as testimony to the truth of the religion in which they occur: they confirm, in other words, *by demonstration* that the faithful are right to belong to this religion rather than another; and as far as any other religion is concerned, these confirming miracles thus become, what Hume calls, 'contrary facts', which establish, as far as the home-religion is concerned, that the truth-claims of any other religion are *false*. But since this is true of all religions – that for any religion A there will always be a religion B that maintains that claims of A to truth are false, and that their own miracles confirm that this is the case – we must conclude that no one religion can ever successfully override another religion's claim to truth by miraculous demonstration. Indeed, since we may assume that the believers of religion A will always be collectively outnumbered by the believers of all other religions – each of them denying that A is the true religion – then the evidence against A being the true religion will always be greater than the evidence that supports it. Thus the experiential evidence provided by miracles of religion A being the true religion will always be outweighed by the experiential evidence provided by other religions that confirms that it is not. This is not to say, of course, that religion A is *not* the only true religion. In any set of contrary beliefs, the logical possibility remains that one of them is true. It is also possible, of course, that all of them are false; but since all these different religions are certified by their own miracles, it is difficult to see how miracles can of themselves guarantee that the claims of their home-religion, unlike all others, are true, particularly when the number of religions may extend to an almost limitless variety, each of them bringing along their own miracles in support.

One way out of this difficulty is to propose, with the theologian John Hick and others, a theory of *religious pluralism*: namely, that all religions are in a sense true, insofar as they are all different responses to one divine reality, embodied in diverse religious traditions, formed under varying historical and cultural situations, and utilizing different images and metaphors. Thus it is not so much that each religion attends to a single ultimate reality as that there is a single ultimate reality to which all religions attend, albeit called by various names (God, Brahman, Allah, Krishna, Dhamma). But this proposal is not successful and does not out-manoeuvre Hume. For a smorgasbord of religions is not possible when their various claims to truth, supported by their confirming miracles, are not merely different but contradictory, i.e., logically antagonistic to the claims of an opposing religion. We need only look at the three great 'religions of the book' to see the extent of these differences. Judaism, Christianity and Islam are all monotheistic, and each believes in an after-life and an elaborate system of rewards and punishments. But Christianity worships a god of three natures (a triune God; the Holy Trinity), whereas Judaism and Islam do not. Islam maintains that Mohammad is the preeminent prophet of Allah, whereas Christianity and Judaism do not. Christianity claims that Jesus of Nazareth is the promised Messiah, which Judaism vehemently denies, while Islam assigns him prophetic status only. These, then, are not merely differences of opinion capable of being grouped together under one roof, but contrary claims, which are logically incompatible. Admittedly some initial coherence may be presumed because all these major religions are theistic; but what then are we to make of the non-theistic religions – e.g., the Samkhya and Mimamsa schools of Hinduism and Theravada Buddhism – which reject altogether the notion of a personal, creator God? It would appear, then, that to overcome the problem of contrariety, as set out by Hume, cardinal features of any particular religion must be relinquished, and this is, as one can imagine, something that many believers are not prepared even to contemplate.[27] So in these cases, Hume concludes, the neutral observer is not unlike a judge hearing a case, in which one set of witnesses discredits the evidence of another set of witnesses: the evidence for one is evidence against the other, and vice versa, and the judge ends up by suspending judgment altogether. For even though each set does agree on one point – that miracles happen – this will mean for the judge, if he be a 'wise man', that no evidence will ever carry sufficient empirical weight to convince him that one religion, and not another, is the one true religion as certified by its miraculous events, since contrary evidence can always be brought to bear by another and opposing religion claiming much the same thing. Thus the claims of both parties to the dispute are to be discounted as 'not proven', to use the Scottish term, no matter how reputable or convinced each set of witnesses is of the truth of their case. To resolve such a dispute as this – for a judge to decide in favour of miracle X in religion A and so against miracle Y in religion

---

27 Among them the so-called 'exclusivists', such as the famous Swiss Protestant theologian Karl Barth (1886-1968), for whom Christianity is the only place where salvation is to be found. It is interesting to note how Hick has changed his own position. Originally converted to fundamentalist Christianity, his advocacy of religious pluralism has, controversially, led him more recently to discard some core Christian beliefs, most notably the literal interpretation of Jesus as the unique incarnation of God. See particularly his contributions to *The Myth of Christian Uniqueness*, ed., with Paul Knitter, London, SCM, 1988.

B – independent evidence would have to be obtained, independent, that is, of the certifying religion, to verify that X had occurred, but not Y. Nor would this be all. For after that, a further link would have to be established between this particular miracle and that particular religion, so that, say, a specified miracle of resurrection in one religion would not be confused with any other opposing (and false) claims to resurrection in any other opposing (and false) religion. But how such evidence could ever be obtained is very hard to see. On this point at least, Hume is unassailable. It is not so much that there are no miracles as that 'a miracle can never be proved, so as to be the foundation of system of religion'.[28]

It is interesting to speculate what Hume would have said if he himself had seen a miracle, if he had been there when Lazarus emerged from his tomb. One can imagine his reply. It is always possible, of course, that what I am seeing is a genuine miracle, and there is nothing in logic which says that a dead man can never come back to life. That I have never seen it happen before is not, then, a logical argument against my seeing it happen now. But having set that possibility aside, I should now ask myself questions as to the probability of this event occurring, setting that probability against the probability of not seeing things as they are. Is it, for example, more likely that what I have seen is the result of natural causes, perhaps even of causes as yet unknown, or less likely? Is it, for example, more likely that I have somehow deceived myself, or been deceived, into believing that Lazarus has genuinely risen from the dead, or less likely? In answer, I should now apply the principle, which operates even in cases of direct eye-witness. This principle reads: the greater the miracle, the less likely it happened This is shorthand for saying that in all cases of this type the full weight of evidence – the innumerable instances when such things have not occurred or have been verified not to occur – will be against the singular evidence of my own senses. The more judicious conclusion, therefore, is that things are not as they appear, and that I have somehow deceived myself or somehow been deceived into believing that Lazarus rose from the dead. Thus, even in this particular case, believing in miracles is never the reasonable thing to do, however reliable the witnesses may be, and even when that witness is myself.

But this is all rather fanciful. Hume never did see a miracle, dismissed all chances of ever seeing one, would strongly doubt whether I had or you had or anybody else had, and would discount entirely the witness-statements of those who said they had. Nor would he require the efforts of a James Randi to support him on this, although doubtless he would be interested in the findings. If the miracles of religion are demonstrations

---

28 *Op.cit.*, p.127.

of divine power, certifying that a being with this power exists, then it is worth remembering that there are far more gods that have died than have ever lived and that these departed gods also performed miracles. In an essay entitled 'Memorial Service' (1922),[29] the famous journalist H.L. Mencken (1880-1956) speaks of the 'graveyard of dead gods', listing well over a hundred of them, all deceased, and all fond of demonstrating their existence and immortality by dramatic and frightening incursions into human affairs: not just by miracles of healing but also by miracles of rage and punishment, by plague, earthquake and sudden death. And even today believers are very parochial in their miracle-claims. While many Roman Catholics regard Padre Piu as a saint endowed with miraculous powers, few Protestants do; and while many Protestants regard Holy Scripture as a living miracle, dictated by God himself, they would almost certainly dismiss as outrageous and slightly ridiculous the claims of Joseph Smith: that it was the angel Moroni who had led him to the discovery of the Book of Mormon, as inscribed on golden plates, on a hill in Wayne County, New York.

There appears, then, to be no *universal* miracle, no permanently inexplicable event which can overcome these parochialisms; one that all religions would embrace. This we may say was rather short-sighted on God's part, causing a lot of distress and bloodshed later on through the inevitable rivalries of religion; but it is certainly understandable why religions should assert their own distinctive creeds. For if a miracle event is said to be permanently inexplicable – inexplicable, that is, in terms of natural laws – then it becomes difficult for a religion to employ the inexplicable as an explanation of its own unique status: that this is an event like no other but one which nevertheless can be said to have a particular origin in the agency and purposes of a particular God. Much better, then, to adopt the opposite route: not to move from miracle to God but from God to miracle. So long, therefore, as the believer can build into his or her own particular notion of God that their God can alone perform miracles, or that this God's miracles are intrinsically superior to those of any other God, there is no need for any verifying evidence to establish that they occur: they now occur by definition, and take their place among the absolute certainties of religious conviction. By this means miracles become no longer independent evidences of God but corroborations of truths already held, forever safeguarded against the scepticism of unbelievers.

---

29 In *A Mencken Chrestomathy: His Own Selection of His Choicest Writing*, New York, Vintage Books, 1982, pp. 95-97. See also *H.L. Mencken on Religion*, ed. S.T. Joshi, Buffalo, N.Y., Prometheus Books, 2002.

7
The Motivations of Belief

i. Introduction

In his *Journal* John Wesley (1703-1791), founder of the Methodist movement, records the following event:

> In the evening I went very unwillingly to a society in Aldersgate Street, where one was reading Luther's preface to the *Epistle to the Romans*. About a quarter before nine, while he was describing the change which God works in the heart through faith in Christ, I felt my heart strangely warmed. I felt I did trust in Christ, Christ alone, for salvation; and an assurance was given me that he had taken away my sins, even mine, and saved me from the law of sin and death. [1]

Wesley's conversion is a model of Christian transformation: datable, emotionally charged, and regenerative in providing a new sense of meaning and purpose. But while the Christian tradition is full of such transformations[2] – the most famous being Paul's conversion on the road to Damascus – it has no monopoly. Quite similar episodes, whether gradual or instantaneous, are to be found not only among all the major religions of the world but also among the less mainstream, with conversions to the Jehovah's Witnesses, Hare Krishna, and the Unification Church, to name but a few. More alarmingly, however, people have also converted to cults that many would regard as downright wicked: to the Branch Dravidian Seventh Day Adventists, made famous by the siege at

---

1   *The Journal of John Wesley*, ed. Nehemiah Curnock, New York, Eaton & Mains, 1909, I, pp.465-78.

2   For a collection of fifty first-person conversion accounts, see *Famous Conversions: The Christian Experience*, ed. Hugh T. Kerr and John M. Mulder, Eerdmans Publishing, 1994. The list starts with Paul the Apostle, includes Augustine, Pascal, Bunyan, Tolstoy, C.S. Lewis and Simone Weil, and finishes with Charles Colson of Watergate fame. For a in-depth analysis of religious conversion, see Lewis R. Rambo, *Understanding Religious Conversion*, Yale, Yale University Press, 1995

John Wesley

Waco, Texas in 1993, or to the People's Temple Movement founded by Jim Jones in 1955 and which in 1978 led to the mass suicide of 918 people in Guyana, or to the Aum Shinrikyo movement, which carried out the sarin gas attack on the Tokyo subway in 1995. All these conversions were doubtless cataclysmic and 'miraculous' experiences for those involved; but their wide-ranging variety reminds us once again how difficult it is to ground any claims to truth upon the particular experiences of particular in-

dividuals operating within a particular religious tradition, no matter how immediate and revelatory these experiences may appear to them. Indeed, all we need do at this point is borrow from the previous chapter Hume's argument against miracles and apply it here. Conversion may be counted among the 'prodigies of religion', and as such it suffers the same fate as other so-called 'contrary facts'. For even if we accept that these unique experiences have a common core, any claim that they are somehow veridical – that they can be employed as confirmations of a particular belief-system – is cancelled out when we find them used to support religious claims that are incompatible with each other. With this Humean critique in mind, it is hardly surprising, then, that the atheist spends little time considering whether conversion-experiences – or indeed any other religious experiences, miraculous or otherwise – can decide between conflicting religious claims or indeed between the devil and God. The answer is that they cannot, and that any move from religious experience to metaphysical conclusion is doomed to failure.

But these objections carry no weight with those who have actually had these experiences, less intense perhaps than the immediate confirmations felt by a Wesley, but nevertheless holding them fast in their belief that beyond this reality there exists another unseen but divine order of being, 'something out there' or a 'near presence' which has been revealed to them. No unique perceptual sensation is offered to support this immediate sense of validity: it is not necessary that any empirical evidence should be provided to warrant this belief in another spiritual universe. It is rather the *feeling itself* that provides its own confirmation and that subsequently acts as the impulse of good conduct, providing what Tolstoy was to call the force 'by which men live'.

It is this subjective element within religion that provides the greatest obstacle to atheism. Atheists may be comfortable in their claim that the so-called 'proofs' of theistic belief have absolutely no intellectual credibility, and that religious

William James

apologists have been completely out-manoeuvred when it comes to their explanations of, say, why people suffer or why they should act morally; but success is much more hard to come by when dealing with the private sensations of faith. And it is not difficult to see why. When believers talk of their religious experiences, they are speaking of an immediate and personal encounter with God, which does not depend on the testimony of others but upon their own privately guaranteed awareness of a divine presence, something they have felt in their innermost being, often overwhelming in its intensity and invariably life-changing, and which is quite sufficient in itself to sweep aside any doubts they may otherwise have had. Besides this, the metaphysical speculations so successfully attacked by atheists seem small beer in comparison and almost irrelevant.

What the atheist is up against at this point can best be appreciated by reference to the work of William James (1842-1910). James' *The Varieties of Religious Experience* (1902) is the undisputed masterpiece of the psychology of religion, and in it he castigates all attempts to demonstrate God's existence either evidentially or by philosophical argument, and dismisses the famous classical 'proofs' as so many 'metaphysical monsters' that have absolutely no bearing on why people come to faith.[3] On what grounds, therefore, do individuals take the momentous decision to believe that there is a God – a decision that will inevitably affect the entire complexion of their lives? James provides the answer in his seminal essay of 1896, 'The Will to Believe'.[4] People embrace religious

---

3   The book is available in many editions; edition used, London and New York, Longmans, Green & Co., 1941.

4   *The Will to Believe and Other Essays in Popular Philosophy*, New York, Dover

belief on 'passional grounds' alone, fully aware that the evidence for
God is 'insufficient', and for that very reason all the more committed
to the stand they have taken. But how, then, do believers know that
their commitment is well placed, that their belief has truth-value and
is not merely, as the atheist will undoubtedly conclude, a psychological
aberration? James' reply is very significant. Religious belief, he maintains,
is *self-verifying*: not in the sense that it can supplant objective information –
if it is raining, no amount of belief in a sunny day will change the climate
– but in the sense that it is true if the belief held has made a verifiable
and concrete difference in the experience of the individual. In other
words, the believer knows that his belief is a true belief when he knows
that it has had a practical effect upon him, that it has had discernible
and real consequences, that it has worked or has 'cash-value' for him. A
belief, in other words, is validated by its *effects*, and this is something that
only the believer can know privately and by introspection. Has this belief
made any actual and appreciable difference to the way I act? If it has,
then it is true for me.

It is interesting to note that a very similar argument is deployed by the
famous psychologist, Carl Gustave Jung (1875-1961), in his influential
account of religious phenomena.[5] He, like James, is quite clear that the
existence of God cannot be proved, and that the classical attempts to
do so are redundant, of antiquarian interest only. All we can be clear
about is that human beings undergo certain psychic experiences – let
us call them 'God-experiences' – and these experiences are immediate,
direct and self-evident. God exists as a psychic reality for such people,
making the statement 'God exists' psychologically true for them in as
much as it is a correct description of a particular psychic event that they
have undergone. As Jung remarks: 'Religious experience is absolute; it
cannot be disputed. You can only say that you have never had such an
experience, whereupon your opponent will reply: 'Sorry, I have'. And
there your discussion will come to an end'.[6] God exists, then, as a psychic
reality, a undeniable and psychologically demonstrable factor within the
believer's own experience, and in affirming his belief he is doing no
more than affirming the truth of his own psychological condition. Thus,
for Jung as for James, the assertion that 'God exists' is not a factual
claim about the existence of an objective reality *apart* from the psychic
experience; it is rather a shorthand expression for the incontestable fact

---

Publications, 1956.

5   I have described Jung's position at length in my *Freud and Jung on Religion*,
London & New York, Routledge, 1997.

6   *Psychology and Religion* (1938), in the *Collected Works of C.G. Jung*, Volume 11,
London, Routledge & Kegan Paul, 1957, 2nd edition 1970, pp. 104-105.

that a particular experience of a particular type has been had, and that this alone is sufficient to provide a warrant for truth. But no additional metaphysical conclusions about whether there is a God or not can be immediately derived from this divine encounter, even though it may well function, as James himself believed, as the root of all religion and the starting-point for the later constructs of creed, doctrine and institutions. What is brought to the believer, then, is psychic, not theological, knowledge – immediate and unerring and operating at the deepest level of his being – and that is enough for him.[7]

Carl Gustave Jung

I do not want to repeat at length here the criticisms that I have already levelled against this type of argument.[8] But it is worth saying again that any experience, however immediate and life-changing, provides no guarantee of truth, if by that James and Jung mean that we may infer from this particular inner psychic experience that it is distinguishable from other mental aberrations: that it is not like the conviction that there really are fairies at the bottom of my garden or that an inner voice has directed me to murder prostitutes. Again, for James and Jung the kind of behaviour initiated by the psychic encounter is essentially *moral in character* – this is the effect which justifies the cause – but even here there is no reason to suppose that a belief known to be false cannot produce desirable moral benefit, as in the case of a preacher cynically utilizing the notion of hell to frighten his congregation into good behaviour. What is false may thus produce the desired benefit.

---

7   Paul Tillich is another who holds a similar position, although in his case he goes to even further extremes. He argues that the psychological experience of being transformed by the New Testament picture of the Christ confirms the man of faith in his belief that it is the real Christ who is portrayed there. For an extended analysis of this argument, see my *Paul Tillich's Philosophy of Art*, Berlin, de Gruyter, 1984, pp.165-172, 206-209.

8   See above, pp.109-111

While, then, the psychic experience may be authoritative for the believer, and while some moral benefit may even accrue from it, the fact that the truth-content of a belief is governed by these factors also means that the same consequences, when flowing from *other beliefs*, provide the self-same guarantee that this belief is also true, however bizarre or repellent that belief may be. It is not just that every major religion becomes an option justified by the same psychic process, but that every sectarian interest, extending down to a membership of one, is similarly justified and elevated to the status of a 'real possibility' by the believer's passional response towards it. The only truth at this point is therefore the truth of the believer's inner psychic experience, and religion has become no more than an expression of this particular condition, but devoid of any cognitive estimate of whether what is believed is true or whether what is held to be true leads to actions that are morally justified.

What concerns us now is not *that* believers have these experiences but *why* they have them. This is a constant puzzle to atheists. What is it that drives people to conclude that their experiences are somehow different and not to be confused with Hume's 'sick men's dreams'? What prompts them to believe that they can somehow reach beyond the normal conditions of life and come into contact with another transcendental reality, which although *unseen* can yet be *described*? – in other words, that these are communicative and informative experiences, peculiar to them and not given to the vast mass of humankind, said to emanate from an all-seeing, benevolent and omnipotent deity, but which they themselves often describe as 'absurd', defying all the norms of rationality. How *do* perfectly normal persons arrive at this quite extraordinary position? Or does the very strength of the feeling encountered here, and the immunity sought, make us suspicious that these are, after all, experiences reducible to the level of natural psychological phenomena, and therefore totally explicable as aberrations of the human spirit: that the gods evoked are no more than the fantasies concocted by men in the image of themselves? It is at this point that atheism flexes its muscles as never before. Religion is now to be reduced to psychopathology, with its roots finally unmasked as a personal and communal evasion of reality, in which human needs are met by the illusory consolations of religion. Here the two outstanding critics are the remaining members of what I have called the 'triumvirate of atheism': Karl Marx and Sigmund Freud.

ii. The Impulse to Believe

The idea that men and women have peopled the world with creatures of their own imagining, and that these creatures should be formalized into representations of good and evil powers, is hardly something new.

More generally known as the 'projection theory', it first finds expression
in ancient Greece, and we have seen this already in the writings of, for
example, Lucretius, Critias the tyrant of Athens, Carneades of Cyrene,
and Pliny the Elder. Indeed, as Bruno Bettelheim makes clear in his study
of the meaning and importance of fairy stories, this projective process is
a familiar one, extending far back through the millennia.

> For a long time in his history man used emotional projections
> – such as gods – born of his immature hopes and anxieties to
> explain man, his society, and the universe; these explanations
> gave him a feeling of security. Then slowly, by his own social,
> scientific, and technological progress, man freed himself of the
> constant fear for his very existence. . . . Translated in terms
> of human behavior, the more secure a person feels within the
> world, the less he will need to hold on to "infantile' projections
> – mythical explanations or fairy-tale solutions to life's eternal
> problems – and the more he can afford to seek rational
> explanations.[9]

In a famous paragraph in *Leviathan* (1651) Thomas Hobbes makes the
same point. Religion originates in a 'fear that proceeds from ignorance',
that, while the gods exist only in the minds of believers, and are but
'creatures of their own fancy', humans 'stand in awe of their own
imaginations'.[10] A century later, and predictably enough, we find David
Hume saying much the same thing in his *The Natural History of Religion*
(1757). The projective process is harshly described as 'the playsome
whimsies of monkeys in human shape', and was first prompted not
by refined speculation but by the much more mundane 'affections of
human life', such as a concern for happiness, the dread of misery, and
the terror of death.[11] And not surprisingly, of course, we find these same
ideas repeated in the overtly atheistic writings of Hume's friend and
contemporary, Baron d'Holbach, in his *System of Nature* (1770):

> These prejudices in man for the marvellous, appear to have been
> the source that gave birth to those wonderful, unintelligible
> qualities with which theology clothed the sovereign of the
> world. The invincible ignorance of the human mind, whose
> fears reduced him to despair, engendered those obscure, vague
> notions, with which he decorated his God.[12]

---

9   *The Uses of Enchantment*, London, Penguin Books, 1976, p.51.
10 *Op.cit.*, Xi, p.26
11 In *David Hume on Religion*, ed. A, Wayne Culver and John Valdimir Price,
    Oxford, The Clarendon Press, 1976, p.32.
12 *The System of Nature*, Volume II, Chapter 2.

a. Ludwig Feuerbach: God as the Projection of Man

Ludwig Feuerbach

However, in the development of the projection theory, pride of place must be given to Ludwig Feuerbach (1804-1872), not least because his work impacts so directly upon the much more sophisticated and influential version of the theory provided by Karl Marx. Feuerbach's classic work is *Das Wesen des Christentums* (1841), translated by George Eliot in 1854 as *The Essence of Christianity*. The central theme of the book may be summarized as *the reduction of theology to anthropology*. Largely in reaction to the idealist philosophy of his teacher at the University of Berlin, G.W.F. Hegel (1770-1831), Feuerbach here develops an atheistic materialism which consists in showing that there is no distinction between divine and human nature – that this distinction is an illusion – and that accordingly what theologians say of God may be transposed into what anthropologists say of man. This transposition demystifies God as man's own invention, as a hypostatization of the human species, in which the divine becomes 'the mirror of man . . . God is for man the commonplace book where he registers his highest feelings and thoughts'.[13]

> Religion is the relation of man to his own nature – therein lies its
> truth and its power of moral amelioration – but to his nature not
> recognized as his own, but regarded as another nature, separate,
> nay, contradistinguished from his own: herein lies its untruth, its
> limitation, its contradiction to reason and morality.[14]

God therefore is the personification of man himself, in which all the most admired human qualities – such as goodness, truthfulness, wisdom, love and justice – are freed from their human source, elevated and then magnified onto a heavenly screen, where they are contemplated and revered as the attributes of a divine being. God, in other words, is humankind writ large, so reducing all metaphysical speculation to no more than constructs of an imagination divorced from reality and mired in illusion and falsehood. To put the matter another way, we can say that religion is

13 *Op.cit.*, New York, Harper Torchbacks, p.63
14 *Ibid.*, p.197.

the expression of an alienated consciousness that cannot grasp its own true self except as a form external to it; or that religious belief involves an immature move away from self-reliance and self-belief towards an infantile need for a father-god, who must be placated if any final rewards are to be achieved. Belief in the next world is thus fuelled by the entirely natural human desire for happiness; but if the desire is real enough, the goal is not, since the after-life is no more than the imagined fulfilment of this desire. Atheism, however, redraws this image of man and restores to him those qualities that properly belong only to him. Man now becomes man's own true god, autonomous and assertive, devoid of any illusions about another realm, and so channelling all his energies into the improvement of himself and of the only world there is – his own. Feuerbach's denial of God should therefore be translated as a denial of the negation of man, or as heralding the advent of man, with the human individual now standing as 'the beginning, the middle and the end of religion.'[15]

b. Karl Marx: Religion as the Opium of the People

Feuerbach's account of how God-concepts are formed in religion is a narrative of the way in which man comes to a knowledge of himself. Religion is relevant as a part – an early part – of the history of his awakening self-consciousness, later to be dispelled as the individual comes to rational maturity and casts aside these fictions of his infancy. With the growing realization that the only way to self-knowledge is through personal experience, the myths of religion are exposed as the realized ideas of human needs, desires and feelings; and, once unmasked, man is released from the tyranny of a judgmental God, and can renew himself as an aspiring and autonomous individual.

For Karl Marx *The Essence of Christianity* remains a central feature in the landscape of his atheism. Friedrich Engels, Marx's principal lieutenant, remarked that, on publication, 'Enthusiasm was general; we all became at once Feuerbachians', and none more so than Marx.[16] Nor indeed does Marx ever depart from the principles first established by Feuerbach: that the objects of religion are illusory and infantile; that they are the products of man's self-alienation from his own true self; and that the first step in the emancipation of human beings was to unmask the deception and deny God. Three years after Feuerbach's book, Marx published his *Critique of Hegel's Philosophy of Right* (1844), and in it he makes no attempt to modify the theory. 'Man', he writes, 'who looked for a superman in the fantastic reality of heaven . . . found nothing there but the *reflexion* of himself",

---

15 *Ibid.*, p.282.

16 Marx is full of praise for Feuerbach in his *Heilige Familie*, where he attributes to him alone the placing of man at the centre of philosophical discussion.

adding that 'The basis of irreligious criticism is: *Man makes religion*, religion does not make man'.[17] But Marx's enthusiasm was short-lived, and as the 1840s advanced he moved decisively away from Feuerbach's optimistic forecast of man's future without religion. What Feuerbach provided, Marx now believed, was an abstract conception of 'Man', a generalized and utopian image of what human beings could become if once released from the illusions of supernaturalism. Feuerbach operates, in other words, as if unmasking the illusion will be sufficient to produce this result, as if the desired social transformation could be achieved by cerebral activity, by an alteration of thought. While Feuerbach was right, therefore, about the mechanisms of projection – on this he is unassailable – he had not asked himself why the delusional images of religion remain so powerful, or why men and women remain alienated and so still in thrall to this fiction of another and better world. It is in order to answer these questions that Marx now turns to an analysis of human society, of the actual day-to-day conditions under which people live, and therefore of those concrete conditions out of which religion has developed. Where Feuerbach claimed to have discovered the secret of theology in anthropology, Marx now seeks to transform anthropology into a realistic sociology or active materialism, which will finally expose the impulses of belief, and so provide a programme for the permanent eradication of religion from society. For once religion is exposed as a derivative of a socio-historical process, then the end of that process will spell the end of religion. The abolition of religion thus becomes a necessary *revolutionary* step and is therefore no longer of theoretical interest only but of a much wider significance in the development of a new humanism.

We move, then, from Feuerbach's speculative philosophy to Marx's much more empirical approach, to his 'new positive science'. This is better known as *historical materialism*. The word 'materialism' here stands for the fact that human nature is governed by the development of material production: that in order to live and to reproduce their kind, individuals must eat, drink, be housed and clothed, and do many other things besides. These demands, however, quickly develop a social complexion as the individual discovers that by cooperation with others his subsistence needs will be better met – that what he cannot provide, others will. So divisions of labour appear, and a two-way relation between human beings and their material environment opens up, in which the crucial role now belongs to the 'mode of co-operation' or to the 'material productive forces' of society. The sum total of these relations of production constitutes the *economic structure of society*, the primitive form

17 'Contribution' to the *Critique of Hegel's Philosophy of Right* (1844), quoted in *Marx and Engels on Religion*, Moscow, Progress Publishers, 1972, p.37.

of which provides the most natural type of human organization: a kind of tribal communism in which each is for all, democratic in character, and devoid of private property, classes or privileged elites.

But paradise doesn't last long. For in the development of these material productive forces, a stage is reached that is ultimately destructive. The division of labour, which in the earliest form operated for universal social benefit, now fragments into a distribution of work and ownership. As the expanding demands (or capacity) of production clash with the contracting controls (or ownership) of production, so we find the formation of groups of individuals – of *classes* – which are defined solely in terms of their material circumstances. The previous exploitation of nature by men is gradually transformed into the exploitation of men by men, and in the ensuing class struggle between opposing economic classes – historically apparent in the divisions between slave owners and slaves, feudal lords and serfs, factory owners and industrial workers – alienation and dysfunction intensify. The division of labour transmutes into the acquisition of private property for some and dispossession for others, and nowhere is this better seen than in advanced capitalist society, where the class struggle reaches fever-pitch. Marx analyses this situation in minute detail in his most famous work, *Das Kapital*, the first volume of which appeared in 1867. A class war now takes place between the capitalist owners of the means of production and the non-propertied or wage-earning workers, the 'proletariat', and is fuelled by the exploitation of the one by the other. We can see this best in the operation of individual labour. For the working man his ability to work has a value in that it provides him with the means of survival, i.e., it equips him with the necessities of life, like food and shelter; but these essentials are only obtained by selling this ability – this is his 'labour-power' – to employers in return for wages. But here the exploitation begins. For while the time spent in maintaining the worker's labour power may be, say, only four hours a day, the actual time spent may last much longer, up to ten hours a day. In the first four hours, therefore, the worker is producing the equivalent of what is paid to him in wages; but for the rest of the time he is producing 'surplus value', a profit that his employer quickly appropriates. Nor is this a matter of choice for the employer. He, too, is subject to the competitive struggle of the market-place; and the surplus-value stolen from the workers enables him to keep afloat, to open up fresh markets and to invest in new factories and machinery. He is therefore forever attempting to increase 'surplus value' by decreasing the wages of his work force or by demanding greater intensity of work or by lengthening the working-day; and all the time, the work force is itself increasing, rarely keeping pace with employment, and so creating a permanent reservoir of job-seekers, which lowers wages still further and keeps the whole under-class in economic dependency. Thus it is that a decreasing number of capitalists usurp and monopolize all the benefits of industrial progress, while the great mass of humankind lives in increasing degrees of misery, oppression, servitude, depravation and exploitation. Under these conditions, it is hardly surprising that individuals become ruined manifestations of humanity, 'alienated' from their intrinsic nature or 'species-being': treated as objects they become objects to themselves, another commodity lacking all dignity or self-worth, with their work no longer an affirmation of themselves but now confronting them as an alien, hostile and external power.

> Within the capitalist system . . . all means for the development of production transform themselves into means of domination over, and exploitation of, the producers; they mutilate the laborer into a fragment of a man, degrade him to the level of an appendage of a machine, destroy every remnant of charm in his work and turn it into a hated toil; they estrange from him the intellectual potentialities of the labor-process . . . they distort the conditions under which he works, subject during the labor-process to a despotism the more hateful for its meanness; they transform his life-time into working-time, and drag his wife and child beneath the wheels of the Juggernaut of capital.[18]

While this picture is one of unremitting gloom, it is, however, precisely this intensification of distress that contributes to the revolutionary transition to communism and the restructuring of society. According to the 'law of increasing misery', the condition of the workers, indeed of almost the entire population, becomes progressively more and more intolerable, and this leads them to combine for their own protection – hence the development of trade unions as centres of resistance – and to the creation of a power which will eventually destroy the whole repressive system. Thus the significance that Marx attaches to the struggle between classes derives from his belief in its historical and inevitable outcome: that the proletariat, now conscious of itself *as a class* with defined interests, is the destined agent of human emancipation; that this is the 'universal class' because its liberation from oppression signals the abolition of all classes and so the emancipation of all humankind. And this liberation, we should stress, is achieved by the very real economic transformation of the socio-material lives of individuals under the conditions of a new mode of production. Both private property and alienated labour are to be abolished, individuals now working not for profit but for the common good – 'from each according to his abilities, to each according to his needs' – so

18 *Capital*, ed. Friedrich Engels, New York, International Publishers, 1967, Vol. I, p.645.

restoring man to himself as a
self-conscious human being.

Thus far I have described
the economic and material
structure of society, what
Marx calls the substructure
(*Unterbau*). Here, to recap,
we find the conflict between
the forces and relations of
production, the growth of
a division of labour and the
consequent development of
a class structure, which is the
primary socio-economic cause
of exploitation and human
alienation, and the abolition of
which is the principal goal of

Karl Marx

revolution. Marx next tells us that upon this material base a superstructure
(*Oberbau*) is constructed, the constituents of which are many and various:
the laws and political institutions of society, the prevailing system of
morality and philosophy, the arts, education and literature. All these are
infused with beliefs and attitudes which Marx describes as *ideologies*, and
which, like everything else in the superstructure, derive directly from the
economic substructure and to that extent not only will reflect the particular
power relations existing there but also and more pertinently will underpin
and legitimate the form of exploitation being practised.

> The ideas of the ruling class are in every epoch the ruling ideas,
> i.e., the class which is the ruling *material* force of society, is at
> the same time its ruling *intellectual* force. The class which has the
> means of material production at its disposal, has control at the
> same time over the means of mental production, so that thereby,
> generally speaking, the ideas of those who lack the means of
> mental production are subject to it. The ruling ideas are nothing
> more than the ideal expression of the dominant material
> relationships, the dominant material relationships grasped as
> ideas; hence of the relationships which make the one class the
> ruling one, therefore, the ideas of its dominance. The individuals
> composing the ruling class . . . rule also as thinkers, as producers
> of ideas, and regulate the production and distribution of the ideas
> of their age: thus their ideas are the ruling ideas of the epoch.[19]

19 *The German Ideology*, pp.64-65.

Ideologies are therefore expressions of exploitative power and as such are illusory or distorted sets of ideas – examples of what Marx calls 'false consciousness' – employed to conceal and excuse the vested interests of the ruling class. Perhaps the best example of this can be seen in the capitalist justification of private property. The so-called right to ownership, while possessed by a few and dispossessing many, is nevertheless enshrined in law, strictly enforced by the courts and the agents of the courts, and philosophically extolled in family and civil society as an expression of individual liberty and enterprise. But the right to property is the right to possess and dispossess simultaneously. A ruling class, therefore, does not have to maintain its dominance solely by coercive force. A much more subtle but equally effective strategic device is to employ the mechanism of ideas; to protect bourgeois self-interest through ideological control, by convincing both master and servant that the status quo is as it should be. But in reality this is another form of enslavement, serving the economic interests of the class in power and so thwarting the revolutionary aspirations of the impoverished underclass.

Once we realize that for Marx *religion is an ideology*, his critique of religion follows straightforwardly enough. Religion is another mechanism of repression, a further fantasy of alienated man and perhaps the most extreme example of a false consciousness. Religion belongs to the superstructure and, to that extent, has no separate or autonomous cultural identity; rather, it has a specific origin and a specific function. The origin of religion lies in the economic substructure, in the system of profit and commerce, of property and exploitation, in the development of class dominance and repression and in the consequent generation of an alienated humanity. In this respect religion is not the cause of a distorted social and economic reality but the effect. Thereafter, however, the function of religion is not to unmask the distortion but to justify it; to act as an apologist of the exploitative order, and this it does by the subtle deployment of ideas. It invents an erroneous dualism between this world and another, fostering the illusion that, while paradise may not be possible here and now, it will be achieved in a glorious after-life: Lazarus inherits but not Dives, and it is with extreme difficulty that the rich man enters the Kingdom of God. An ultimate balancing of the books is thus promised, with the poor man now achieving in heaven what was denied him on earth. But this pernicious but consoling falsehood masks a diversionary tactic. Rather than rousing individuals to transform their world here and now, religious belief inspires them to take flight into another fantastical realm. Thus the revolutionary impulse for change is muted by the soporific of religion.

> The basis of irreligious criticism is: *Man makes religion*, religion does not make man. . . . But *man* is no abstract being squatting outside the world. Man is *the world of man*, the state, society. This state, this society, produces religion, a *reversed world-consciousness*, because they are *a reversed world*. . . . The struggle against religion is therefore mediately the fight against *the other world*, of which religion is the spiritual *aroma*. *Religious* distress is at the same time the *expression* of real distress and the *protest* against real distress. Religion is the sigh of the oppressed creature, the heart of a heartless world, just as it is the spirit of a spiritless situation. It is the *opium* of the people[20]

We are now in a better position to appreciate the distinctive form of Marx's atheism. Feuerbach, we recall, although substantially correct in his diagnosis of the mechanism of projection, could provide no explanation of why religion, even when unmasked as a disrupted form of consciousness, should yet retain its hold upon the popular imagination. Marx now provides the answer. Feuerbach had failed to see that religion is a socio-economic product, that indeed all the products of the human mind are derivatives of material conditions. Feuerbach had accordingly focused his criticisms in the wrong direction: at the fantastical images that religion produces but not at the socio-economic framework upon which they depend. Thus Feuerbach considers human beings outside the context of those social conditions that actually shape and change individual consciousness, and so does not realize that the fictions of religion are themselves products of material-economic circumstances; and that these circumstances, moreover, are themselves distorted and not natural. By contrast, what Marx reveals is that the impulse to believe is rooted in the actual exploitation of human beings under the material conditions of life – that the process of alienation that produces the illusions of another world is tied irretrievably to the process of alienation that human beings experience under the everyday social conditions of labour. Since therefore religion feeds upon economic and social deprivation, the abolition of religion will only be achieved by a *political* reversal of these distorted material conditions, by the emancipation of work from capitalist exploitation and surplus-labour. The overthrow of God as a class-of-one thus coincides with the overthrow of all classes in a new type of classless society, with the abolition of private property and the conquest of human self-alienation.

---

20 'Contribution' to the *Critique of Hegel's Philosophy of Right, op.cit.*, pp.37-38. An additional note: Lenin in 1905 writes that 'Religion is opium for the people. Religion is a sort of spiritual booze, in which the slaves of capital drown their human image, their demand for a life more or less worthy of man.' *Lenin Collected Works*, Moscow, Progress Publishers, 1965, p.83

> Atheism as the supersession of God is the emergence of
> theoretical humanism, and communism as the supersession of
> private property is the indication of real human life as man's
> property, which is also the emergence of practical humanism. In
> other words, atheism is humanism mediated with itself through the
> supersession of religion, and communism is humanism mediated
> with itself through the supersession of private property.[21]

Marx is unique among the atheists that we have discussed so far because he alone provides a formula for the end of religion. This, to stress again, is to be achieved not by the philosophical unravelling of the illusions of belief but by tracing those illusions to their substructural and economic source and by there administering a social and political adjustment, revolutionary in form and scope. Deeds rather than words are therefore called for, as Marx makes clear in the famous eleventh proposition in the *Theses on Feuerbach* (1845): 'The philosophers have only *interpreted* the world, in various ways; the point is to *change* it'.[22] Marx's atheism, therefore, goes beyond a mere reduction of society's religious life to its material life and offers additionally a practical means – a revolutionary *praxis* – for the total eradication of religion. The impulse to believe in a heavenly society is rooted in the material and class-divided life of the earthly society; and once this is understood – that religion is the ideology of economically or politically dominant exploiting classes – then the actual elimination of class divisions will inevitably spell the actual elimination of the ideology it spawns. Religion is perhaps the most powerful weapon in the armoury of alienation, both a cause of it and its expression: it advances a false metaphysic, propagates a false morality and hinders the liberation of the exploited. But all this will disappear with the overthrow of the capitalist mode of production and the abolition of a society based on class antagonisms. 'The abolition of religion as the *illusory* happiness of the people is required for their *real* happiness. The demand to give up the illusions about its condition is *the demand to give up a condition which needs illusions*'.[23]

Marx's atheism is the most influential ever devised; and I say this only because for the greater part of the twentieth century a considerable percentage of the world's population upheld the communist creed and so accepted atheism as part of their general system of belief. However, in its political application it has proved to be fairly disastrous, and with the collapse of Soviet communism in the 1990s the Marxist philosophy has, unsurprisingly, come under increasing scrutiny. The weaknesses of

---

21 *1844 Manuscripts: Early Texts*, quoted by David McLellan, *The Thought of Karl Marx*, London, Macmillan, 1972, pp.216-217.

22 *Op.cit.*, p.123

23 'Contribution' to the *Critique of Hegel's Philosophy of Right* (1844), *op.cit.*, p.38.

the system are indeed fairly
apparent, not least in its
claim that the victory of the
proletariat is both inevitable
and the agent of permanent
social reform – and thus by
implication the nemesis of
religion. Neither proposition
can be sustained. Bourgeois
society has proved to be
remarkably resilient and no
major social revolution has
occurred in the advanced
capitalist countries of Britain,
France, Germany or the
United States. On the other
hand, communist revolutions
have occurred in countries
with largely agricultural eco-

Karl and Jenny Marx

nomies: in Russia in 1917, in the former Yugoslavia in 1945, and in China
in 1949. We should further note that where the proletariat has advanced
to power, it has hardly been a paragon of virtue and has tended to create
oppressive regimes of its own, whose economic exploitation of other
classes has been fully the match of anything to be seen in the capitalist
systems of labour. And finally one must question Marx's central claim
that it is the material substructure of society that entirely governs the
social, political and spiritual processes of the superstructure, so that the
slightest change in the one will directly impact on the other. Even at
the time this economic reductionism was questioned by Marx's closest
associate, Frederick Engels, who believed in a much more reciprocal
relationship, one which would allow, for example, that developments
in mathematics, science and education could affect economic output
– a fairly uncontentious assumption, I should have thought. Indeed,
the social theorist Max Weber (1864-1920), in his *The Protestant Ethic
and the Spirit of Capitalism* (1904-5) goes even further and reverses the
relationship entirely, arguing that it was the Protestant theology of
salvation that brought about the capitalistic exploitation of labour, and
not, as the Marxist schema would require, the other way round.

All of which brings into question at least one strand of Marx's theory
of religion: that by the institution of new socialist relationships, in which
private property has been eliminated as a source of exploitation, religion
will lose its roots and cease to be. Marxist literature in general has always

made much of the fact that the rise and spread of Christianity is almost entirely due to the deplorable living conditions in the Roman Empire at the end of the first century, that the early Christians practised a form of common ownership, and that gradually this religion of the poor metamorphosized into a reactionary ally of the rich. So Marx speaks of the social principles of Christianity justifying the slavery of antiquity, the serfdom of the Middle Ages, and most pertinently the oppression of the proletariat; and Engels, in similar vein, maintains that whenever religion becomes institutionalized it generates repressive clerical hierarchies, as evidenced by the treatment of the Hussites and Anabaptists in sixteenth-century Germany.[24] Another and rather pertinent example is provided by the historian Michael Bordeaux. He points out that the Moscow Patriarchate, which was formed by Stalin as the central body of the Russian Orthodox Church, overtly subscribed to every military initiative of the Soviet regime: the suppression of the Hungarian uprising in 1956, the erection of the Berlin Wall in 1961, and the invasions of Czechoslovakia and Afganistan in 1968 and 1979.[25] But this picture is not all of a piece, and there are other cases in which working-class rebellion against industrial capitalism was inspired, rather than thwarted, by the Church. It is sufficient to give only one example. Roman Catholic 'liberation theology', which began in Latin America during the 1960s – later to be exported to the United States as Black Liberation – developed a programme of wealth redistribution and class realignment, which consciously incorporated Marx's analysis of economic exploitation and which placed the priest at the forefront as the spokesman of the poor.[26]

If religion cannot therefore be *a priori* associated with exploitation, then it cannot be assumed as a matter of historical necessity that the end of exploitation spells the end of religion. At best, the obliteration of belief from the cultural map forms part of a general prediction that a particular form of integrated society will evolve at some time in an unspecified future as the result of a particular class revolution, with religious authorities

---

24 'The Peasant War in Germany', *Marx and Engels on Religion, op.cit.*, pp.86-105
25 'Russia' in the *Encyclopedia of Politics and Religion*, London, Routledge, 1998, p.657.
26 So the Peruvian theologian Gustavo Gutierrez, a leading figure of the movement: 'There can be authentic development for Latin America only if there us liberation from the domination exercised by the great capitalist countries, and especially the most powerful, the United States.' *A Theology of Liberation*, 1973, p.88. For Black Liberation see James H. Cone, *Black Theology of Liberation*, 1970. Pope Benedict XVI, when Prefect of the Congregation for the Doctrine of the Faith, denounced Liberation Theology as a 'singular heresy', describing it as a 'fundamental threat' to the Church and prohibiting many of its leading proponents from speaking publicly.

placed firmly on the side of the capitalist oppressors. If Marx's critique of religion were no more than this, and was confined solely to these utopian prophecies of imminent bourgeois collapse, no place would be reserved for him among the pantheon of atheists. Indeed, it could even be argued that his position is not even inherently atheistic, given that all he is rejecting is a perversion of religion arising from a defective but transient social order.

But there is a second and altogether more potent strand to his atheism, which cannot be so easily dismissed. This has to do with Marx's account of *alienation*. His view is that alienation is an expression of an inhuman state of affairs, and more particularly that human self-estrangement follows from man perceiving himself to be – and actually being – *a unit of labour*. Once we leave aside Marx's belief that overcoming alienation is certain and assured by the victory of the proletariat, we are left with an analysis of human beings as they actually function in everyday life and without the prospect of any immediate social emancipation. This is the arena of individuals caught within the web of unremitting work, so placed that they are incapable of reconciling themselves to what they have become. Marx describes the alienated individual in various modes: alienated from others, alienated from his work and the products he makes, only marginally happier at home, with no hope of release. Particular prominence is given to alienation from 'species-being' (*Gattungswesen*), a concept implicit in all forms of self-estrangement. By way of explanation Marx employs the age-old distinction between *essence* and *existence*. Species-being is the individual's *essence* as an autonomous and conscious producer, who through creative activity both transforms inanimate nature and himself: in this sense the world becomes a reflection of his own being, bearing the stamp of his unique individuality and values. For Marx, then, the wonder of human beings lies in their capacity to create so much, to live beyond the requirements of mere subsistence, and to humanize their world. Their tragedy, on the other hand, is that under the actual conditions of *existence* this creative human essence remains unrealized. For in reality people have to work in order to live and not to create, have to labour ceaselessly for products that belong to others and not to them, and have to compete against each other rather than to cooperate for the common good. This is the grubby and impoverished world of wage labour so graphically described in the works of Marx's great contemporary, Charles Dickens (1812-1870) who, in such novels as *Hard Times* (1854) and along with many other Victorian writers of the period, 'have issued to the world more political and social truths than have been uttered by all the professional politicians, publicists and moralists put together'.[27]

27 'The English Middle Class' (1854) in *Marx Engels on Literature and Art*, Moscow, Progress Publishers, 1976, p. 43.

This concept of alienation gives us a much richer platform upon which to appreciate Marx's atheism. The affirmation of God as a being distinct from and superior to man constitutes *a denial of human autonomy*, and thus is a specific expression of alienation from species-being. The wish to live the religious life, to live subserviently in the shadow of a superior being, entails therefore the further dehumanization of the individual, a loss of his freedom to act, and so of any chance to find fulfilment in his work and social relationships. Religion, that is, presents man as a debased currency, reducing him to the level of merchandise, as the property of God, once again related to his own activity only as fettered activity under the domination of another. So theology re-doubles the alienation already experienced in the workplace, substituting a capitalist exploiter for a divine one.

We arrive, then, at the original source of individual unhappiness and alienation. Human beings are enslaved by an ideological illusion of their own making, and the impulses of religion are now unmasked as so many acts of escape from the real processes of life. But within the framework of this ideological illusion lies the seed of its own undoing. This too takes place within *the sphere of labour*, that is, within the perspective of productive and creative work as an expression of human self-affirmation. The transition from a state of inauthentic and dysfunctional existence under God to a life of authentic existence within the community of workers is effected by the re-assertion by the individual of his own property rights over himself, by which he can *make himself for himself and others*. In this sense atheism is a proclamation of the independence of man, of man as the only absolute: it stands as the necessary antidote to the opiates of religion, and liberates man to self-fulfilment, which is *to realize by his own efforts his essential being within existence*. For Marx, as we have seen, this conjunction of essential and existential being is actually achievable within communist society. In this Marx's optimism is almost certainly misplaced if only because it places too heavy a weight upon the proletariat as the agent of universal emancipation. But whether realizable or not, Marx contends that this secular form of salvation cannot be counted an illusion in the way that the religious counterpart is an illusion. No other transcendental world is postulated other than the empirical world of known reality, and Marx's optimism is emphatically practical and anchored exclusively in rational and humanistic belief in the efficacy of productive work. When therefore any human being takes flight into religious fantasy – whenever indeed, even today, believers point to a resurgence of religious feeling in any given society – we should look to the nature of alienation from whence it comes: to the class poverty of economic exploitation, to the brutal process of dehumanization that results, and to the sense of desperation that each powerless and isolated individual feels when living within the alien world of unrestricted consumerism.

c. Sigmund Freud: Religion as a Universal Obsessional Neurosis

For Marx the impulse of religious belief expresses an individual's inner need to assert his authentic self and to overcome capitalist alienation, which has reduced him to the level of another expendable commodity. This conclusion may well strike a chord in our credit-crunch world, and Marx, I feel sure, would be unsurprised by any resulting upsurge in religious fervour as people turn away from the economic disappointments of earth to the securities of heaven. Religion remains, however, a remedial affliction, which, until its final eradication, will always divert human beings away from their proper duties towards themselves and their world.

It is interesting to note that, if we look at the final pages of Sigmund Freud's account of religion, we find almost exactly the same conclusion. Men and women should be 'educated to reality' – the reality being that there is no God and that this is the only world there is – and that once they are educated to see religion for what it is – an illusion – there will be a greater chance of social progress. Here, however, Freud is considerably less optimistic that Marx. He accepts that this hope may also be an illusion; but he believes that this experiment in 'irreligious education' is still worth attempting.[28] This cautionary note indicates that Freud, unlike Marx, makes no predictions of ultimate success. He acknowledges that religion is a bitter-sweet drug that has infected people since childhood, and that many individuals are quite incapable of breaking the habit. The impulse to believe does not derive, then, from any external agency but is an *internal and psychological affliction*. He agrees with Marx that it is a curable affliction, but one that can only be cured by an act of introspection and not, as Marx prescribes, by some adjustment of social conditions: individuals, in other words, must lay bare the hidden impulses of their innermost being, assisted only by the methods of psychoanalysis.

Freud begins by taking note of a curious feature of religious activity: that the behaviour exhibited bears a striking similarity to the behaviour of the obsessional neurotic. Hours are spent carrying out certain rituals, which have a ceremonial and compulsive importance, becoming almost

---

28 *The Future of an Illusion*, The Penguin Freud Library, 12, p.233. All references to Freud will be taken from the Penguin edition. The following account relies heavily on my own *Freud and Jung on Religion*, London & New York, Routledge, 1997, and I am grateful to the publishers for permission to quote extensively from it.

'sacred acts', and feelings of guilt invariably accompany any deviation from them, however trivial. As an initial diagnosis, it would appear, then, that these rituals are designed to ward off certain instinctual impulses and to prevent the punishments that will come if one succumbs to them. But what can these instinctual impulses be? In answer we must turn to a more general account of the Freudian concept of neurosis, comprised of two principal components: repression and the Oedipus complex.

Freud never departs from the view – indeed this is the most important assumption of all psychoanalytic theory – that there are certain unconscious mental processes which cause disorders that could not otherwise be explained away as the result of organic disease. The disorder that first drew Freud's attention to this was hysterical paralysis, and in collaboration with his early associate, Josef Breuer, he drew up an initial explanation in the *Studies on Hysteria* of 1895. The conclusion was that hysterics suffered 'mainly from reminiscences', i.e., that hysteria is provoked by the recollection of traumas considered painful or shameful but which have somehow become locked within the unconscious mind. The mechanism that prevents this from happening is known as *repression*, which Freud was later to call the 'corner-stone' of psychoanalysis. Repression is a form of forgetting but sufficiently powerful to prevent these past memories from issuing from the unconscious into the conscious mind. Unknown to the individual, therefore, a constant war is in progress and it is from this conflict that 'neurotic' disorders arise. The past emotion cannot be discharged and so channels itself into the production of neurotic symptoms, into the appearance of hysterias, obsessions, phobias and anxieties.

The next step was to determine whether all forms of trauma have a common characteristic. It was not until 1905, with the publication of his *Three Essays on Sexuality*, that Freud concluded that the nucleus of every case of neurosis was the repression of an innate *sexual instinct* – to which Freud gave the generic name 'libido' – and more precisely the repression of a specific libidinal relation, common to every individual, namely, that between the child and its parents. This is characterized by an emotional attachment to the parent of the opposite sex and an attitude of rivalry to the parent of the same sex. The complex here formed is famously called the *Oedipus complex* – its name derived from the Greek legend of King Oedipus, who killed his father and married his mother.

We are now able to give a more exact description of a neurosis. Within the repressed trauma lies a sexual component, sufficiently threatening that the individual represses it. What is repressed is now revealed to be an Oedipal impulse – the desire for incest for the mother and hatred of the father. It is these two instinctual impulses which, although normal parts of every childhood, are expelled from the consciousness, repressed into the unconsciousness, but which force their way back into consciousness in the abnormal outlet of the symptoms of neurosis. Now once we realize that every account of neurosis has this general format, we can immediately draw some conclusions about religion. For if religion is also a neurosis it too must have its origin in the suppression of the sexual or libidinal impulse. More exactly, the beginnings of religion can be explained in terms of the Oedipus complex.

Sigmund Freud in 1907

When a boy, from the age of two or three, has entered the phallic phase of his libidinal development, is feeling pleasurable sensations in his sexual organ and has learnt to procure these at will by manual stimulation, he becomes his mother's lover. He wishes to possess her physically in such ways as he has divined from his observations and intuitions about sexual life, and he tries to seduce her by showing her the male organ which he is proud to own. In a word, his early awakened masculinity seeks to take his father's place with her; his father has hitherto in any case been an envied model to the boy, owing to the physical strength he perceives in him and the authority with which he finds him clothed. His father now becomes a rival who stands in his way and whom he would like to get rid of. If while his father is away he is allowed to share his mother's bed and if when his father returns he is once more banished from it, his satisfaction when his father disappears and his disappointment when he emerges again are deeply felt experiences. This is the subject of the Oedipus complex, which the Greek legend has translated from the world of a child's fantasy into pretended reality. Under the conditions of our civilization it is invariably doomed to a frightening end.[29]

---

29 'An Outline of Psychoanalysis' (1940), *Penguin Freud Library* (1986) 15, pp. 423-424.

In addition to the innumerable case-studies that Freud brings forward in support of his theory – of which the most famous are the cases of Little Hans, the Wolf Man, the Rat Man and Judge Schreber – Freud's claim is given a further and more detailed anthropological twist when he turns to consider the origins of religion in his *Totem and Taboo*, a collection of four essays published in 1907. Freud begins by noting that, perhaps unexpectedly, primitive people like the aborigines of Australia have very strict attitudes about sex, none more so than the 'taboo' about incest. Indeed, so great is this taboo that it has led to a system known as 'exogamy', which requires that sexual partners must be found outside the tribe. This system of sexual restriction is further linked to another feature of primitive religion: totemism. A totem is a sacred object, usually an animal or plant, which the tribe regards as their guardian spirit or oracle, which is also taboo in the sense that it must not be killed or eaten: it is further regarded as the clan's common ancestor, which means that all members become one single family. This totemic kinship further explains exogamy, since now any sexual relations within the group become effectively incestuous.

Strict prohibitions surround the taboo of incest or the taboo surrounding the totem, and any infringement will lead to disaster: any person who breaks a taboo becomes taboo himself and taboos can only be lifted through certain ceremonial acts, like washing. And from this Freud draws an important psychological conclusion, not usually found in the manuals of anthropology. The only explanation for why taboos are so stringently avoided is because unconsciously these are precisely the things that are most *desired*. These taboos thus incorporate a condition known as 'ambivalence': the desire to do what is forbidden. To impose a taboo is thus to renounce something that one wishes for, and this explains why the punishments are so drastic. The further fact that the most ancient taboos are those governing incest and the killing of the totem suggest that these incorporate the most powerful and primitive of desires.

This argument is given further historical support in what is the most famous section of *Totem and Taboo*, in which Freud presents his re-working of Darwin's primal horde theory. Exogamy was practised amongst primitive men as a practical consequence of the fact that originally they lived in small groups presided over by a dominant male, who possessed many wives and children. His position could only be maintained by driving the younger males out of the tribe to find mates, so that the young females could mate only with him. Owing therefore to the jealousy of the powerful father, there was a prohibition upon sexual intercourse, which, with the development of totemism, became a rigorously enforced totemic regulation. But significantly the position of the dominant male was not unassailable. Overcome with jealousy and sexual frustration, the sons collaborated to kill and eat their father – they were cannibals, after all – but were soon overcome by guilt for what they had done, and so, failing individually to take over their father's position, they banded together into a clan of brothers and once again turned to the practice of exogamy – so removing the original motive for killing their father – and created a father-substitute in the form of the totem. The yearly celebration of the totem meal was, therefore, nothing less than the solemn commemoration of the original crime, the murder of the father.

It is not difficult to see where Freud's argument is heading: the totemic system is a product of the conditions involved in the Oedipus complex. In other words, in totemism we find the beginnings of religion, and at the heart of totemism stands mankind's earliest festival, the totem meal, which is nothing less than the repetition and ritual remembrance of the original criminal act. Psychoanalysis has therefore revealed that, at inception, religion contains the nucleus of every case of neurosis. For if the totem animal is the father, then the two great taboos of totemism – the taboo against incest and the taboo against killing the totem animal – have here coincided with the two great crimes of Oedipus: getting rid of the father and taking the mother to wife.

> Features were thus brought into existence which continued thenceforward to have a determining influence on the nature of religion. Totemic religion arose from the filial sense of guilt, in an attempt to ally that feeling and to appease the father by deferred obedience to him. All later religions are seen to be attempts at solving the same problem.[30]

We should next ask how totemic religion developed into the belief in a God. This occurs in the following way. Not one of the murderous sons has the power to become like their father, and this inability leads to a desperate longing for the father-ideal, which increases over time as their original hostility towards their father decreases. This first expresses itself in the veneration felt for certain human individuals, but which gradually transmutes into the creation of gods. Gods are therefore revivals of the paternal ideal, an elevation to godhead of the murdered father. Nowhere is this better seen than in Christianity, where the original sin against God the Father is taken to be so great that it can only be atoned for by the sacrifice of the Son. But even here the law of ambivalence remains. The act which commemorates the father's murder – the totemic meal now transposed into the eating of flesh at the Eucharist – is the very act by which the Son displaces the Father and achieves a victory over him. So the Father-religion of Judaism becomes the Son-religion of Christianity.

---

30 *Totem and Taboo*, p. 206

This completes the first part of Freud's account of religion, and one important feature of it should be highlighted. All religious people are obsessive neurotics and at the heart of their neurosis stands an unresolved Oedipus complex; but, as has now been made clear, this complex and the guilt it generates are not merely situations that every human being passes through – in the relation of every son to every father and mother – it is also something *inherited*, something that is passed down through the generations but first experienced among the sons of the primal horde. Freud expresses this in the use of two terms: *ontogeny* and *phylogeny*. Ontogeny has to do with the individual organism and phylogeny with the species. So the Oedipus complex can be expressed as follows: it is the personal (and ontogenetic) repetition of something that is embedded within the unconscious mind, namely, the universal (and phylogenetic) experience of the killing of the father. This makes the Oedipus complex particularly potent and impossible to avoid: it is both an experience of each individual's libidinal life and a birthright, something first acquired in the life of the primal horde.

This conclusion, as we shall discover, figures prominently in the second part of Freud's analysis of religion. This introduces us to his most widely-read book on the subject, written in 1927: *The Future of an Illusion*. First we should distinguish an illusion from a delusion. A delusion is something clearly false, a contradiction of reality; an illusion, on the other hand, has more to do with human wishes and the motivations of belief. Illusions, therefore, set little store by observation and verification but are concerned more with inner convictions and thus have a more psychical origin and are rooted in the strength of the wishes they contain. In saying, then, that *religion is an illusion* Freud is not saying that its beliefs are necessarily false but rather that their power lies in their unique provision of a unique set of satisfactions which the human psyche desires above all things, offering 'fulfillments of the oldest, strongest and most urgent wishes of mankind. The secret of their strength lies in the strength of those wishes'.[31]

What, then, are these wishes? When specifying the first of them, Freud makes no pretence to originality and treads the familiar path of the projection theory. The gods are the personifications of the natural forces that threaten humankind – storms, floods, disease – and these acts of imagination give human beings a measure of control: the beings so created can be appeased and bribed and so robbed of part of their power. By humanising nature in this way, our happiness can be increased by assuming some control over our unhappiness. Even the painful riddle of death may be overcome by the hope of an after-life.

---

31 *The Future of an Illusion*, p.212

In this way religion provides an answer to *external* suffering, of what can happen to human beings when at the mercy of the alien forces of the natural world; but it also provides an answer to *internal* suffering, and here psychoanalysis comes into its own. We have already seen the power of the sexual instincts – amongst which Freud counts incest, cannibalism and a lust for killing – and it is easy to imagine what would happen to civilized living if these wishes went unbridled. So it is a social requirement, necessary for the preservation of civilization itself, that human beings do not succumb to their instincts but rather bend their desires to the conventions of society, which, in the moral commands of religion, prohibit sexual intercourse outside marriage and impose the law of abstinence. This, however, is to thwart the natural power of the libido and in consequence repression and neurosis occur on a grand scale, and we find the sexual instinct, by the process known as sublimation, redirected into some activity of social or ethical importance, into, for example, service to the community and charitable works. But even these sublimations cannot entirely assuage the desires of the libidinal instinct. Compliance, then, with the demands of civilized society does not have the desired liberating effect and the moral restrictions imposed by religion, far from providing genuine fulfilment, breed only frustration, resentment, and, most important of all, an acute sense of guilt that what one most desires is forbidden or, to use an earlier terminology, 'taboo'. Once again, therefore, we encounter the full force of the emotional entanglements of 'ambivalence', now placed within a social context and fostered by the well-meaning prohibitions of religion. For while, on the one hand, the laws of society and religion protect the individual from the full force of the sexual desires that threaten his civilized world, they prevent, on the other hand, the achievement of those desires and so act as an extreme form of repression, energizing the neuroses. It is small wonder, then, that now the two attractions of religion combine to produce the most extreme form of compulsive neurotic disorder: *the longing for the father-figure*. For in this particular desire we find both the desire for a providential and benevolent god, powerful enough to protect us from the terrors of the external world, and we also find the acute psychic longing for an actual father, the father of every individual's Oedipal history and therefore of the accumulated guilts inherited both from his distant ancestral past and from his own immediate familial experiences.

We can now appreciate why the religious image of the Father-God has such an obsessional hold upon believers. At one level it fulfils a basic need of humanity by relating to an authority sufficiently powerful to protect us from the natural elements; but this alone would be insufficient to account for the compulsive character of belief. For this to be explained we must understand that the belief has undergone the psychic process of repression, that embedded within it are other feelings associated with the father-image, and that these feelings are feelings of *guilt* originating from two memories: from the memory of each individual's guilty relation to his own father and from the memory arising from every individual's remorse for the primal crime: the murder of the father by the sons of the primal horde. Religion, to repeat, is wish-fulfilment, but the wishes are those derived from the fantasies of the infantile mind as it represses its libidinal and ambivalent instincts in relation to the dominant male. A sense of guilt thus becomes the most important ingredient in the development of religion and it accounts for all the rituals and ceremonies associated with it, which are rigorously upheld and produce an acute sense of anxiety when omitted. They bear the hallmark, therefore, of all compulsive and obsessional behaviour, which, in this particular case, is designed to placate the father we have offended and, if possible, to avert the punishment we have deserved. Religion is therefore a fantasy born of a thirst for filial obedience and of a desire to avert the punishments which would otherwise be visited upon us for having the instincts we have. Religion, as Marx expresses it in a memorable phrase, is like all neurotic illness, a symptom of the 'return of the repressed.'[32]

Like Marx before him Freud concludes his analysis with an appeal to put aside these childish illusions. Obeisance before the father is by definition an *infantile activity*, and should be discarded as the individual grows to maturity. This process is invariably uncomfortable and not everyone makes this transition to adulthood, preferring to remain within the securities of the parental home. But the fact that many feel like this, and remain stuck in the illusions of childhood, does not mean that all do. There are therefore those who have given up the intoxicants of religion and in so doing have been thrown back on their own resources. In this way they will now be able to concentrate their liberated energies on improving the human lot on earth without the distractions of heaven, thereby hopefully achieving 'a state of things in which life will become tolerable for everyone and civilization no longer oppressive to anyone'.[33]

The similarity between Marx and Freud does not, however, stop here. In both cases this orientation away from religion is part of a more general *scientific outlook*: that knowledge must proceed from verifiable observation and that any other sources – such as revelation, intuition or ideology – must be rejected. In Marx's case, the conclusion that religion is an exploitative mechanism is drawn from an empirical (and economic) study

---

32 *Moses and Monotheism*, Penguin Books, Harmondsworth, 1990, p.323.
33 *Ibid.*, p. 233.

of classes, and in Freud's case, the conclusion that religion is a neurosis is drawn from an empirical (and psychoanalytic) study of repression. Implicit in both is a fairly rigid determinism: that everything operates according to the principle of universal causation - that every event has a cause; and that once the cause has been isolated and removed the effect will duly follow. So exploitation is the direct and predictable consequence of the material conditions of life, and the symptoms of neurosis the direct and predictable consequence of an original oedipal trauma; and in each case to eradicate

Sigmund Freud in 1938

the cause is to eradicate the effect. But the principle that nothing can be true unless verified by experimental research does not hold in religion. Rather, the flight into fantasy occurs within a self-contained and inviolable system of doctrine and evades refutation by never submitting its hypotheses to the cold light of verifiable experience.

Freud therefore joins with Marx in claiming that his critique of religion derives power from the criterion of truth, namely, the reality-principle that nothing can be held to be true unless it corresponds with the external world. But this is a principle to which – again like Marx before him – Freud himself does not always adhere. Indeed the catalogue of error is extensive, a detailed account of which I have provided elsewhere.[34] We need only note here the following points, starting with the fact that there is almost no evidence for the existence of the primal horde – a theory itself built around a Darwinian footnote – and that research into the lives of our primitive ancestors does not find the degree of aggression required to support the hypothesis of an original murder. Nor is there any substantial evidence for the institution of the totemic meal and sacrifice, upon which, we recall, Freud bases his theory that this is nothing less than a commemoration of the original parricide. Further still, even if

34 *Freud and Jung on Religion*, pp.60-81.

all these historical incidents could be supported, the transmission of the guilt of the sons down the subsequent generations would require a belief in the discredited Lamarckian thesis that acquired characteristics may be inherited – a theory that even Freud's most ardent supporters largely rejected at the time. Perhaps most surprising of all, the Oedipus complex – the discovery of which Freud regarded as his supreme achievement, on a par with the discovery of the wheel – cannot be given the central place that Freud reserves for it. For while there is no doubt that some young children do have sexual feelings towards their parents, there is no evidence to support the view that all do. This immediately undermines the theory that the Oedipus complex is the kernel of neurosis and the *universal* phenomenon of all psychic life. This being the case, it cannot be claimed that *every* religious act is compulsive and obsessional because it embodies a particular kind of guilt associated with the repression of an infantile libidinal instinct. Many other criticisms can be levelled against Freud's theory of religion; but these are, I think, sufficient to repudiate the claim that God exists only as a projection of Oedipal desires. Again, it is worth noting that even many of his distinguished contemporaries – the most notable being Carl Gustav Jung – did not support Freud on this point and went on to construct psychological theories entirely sympathetic to religion.

Yet, despite all these fairly obvious weaknesses, Freud retains a unique place within the history of atheism; and setting aside the generalities of his sexual theory – not least in his tortuous convolutions to provide a female equivalent to the Oedipus complex – or the embarrassments of many of his historical and anthropological constructions, Freud's achievement remains intact. Freud was not the discoverer of the unconscious mind, but he was the first to use it as the scientific formula of diagnostic explanation, providing a wealth of clinical observation to support his central proposition: that the pathogenic repression of negative or traumatic material – or what many modern psychotherapists more neutrally call 'cognitive avoidance' – is the determinative factor in the creation of neurotic illness and of the delusions that accompany it. Unsurprisingly, with this tool in their armoury, many atheists have been quick to apply the Freudian methodology to a whole range of religious beliefs. One can by this means venture to resolve the Myth of Paradise as an infantile desire for a desexualized innocence; the Myth of the Fall as the guilt resulting from libidinal repression; and the Myth of Judgement Day as the inevitable unmasking of these natural impulses and the punishment for having them by a divine disciplinarian. Similarly and by the same method belief in an after-life becomes not merely an extension of narcissism but the necessary stage for a final acting out of the infantile (and ambivalent) desire for both approval and punishment. Thus metaphysics is easily converted into metapsychology, into the pathology of the return of the repressed.[35] Less programmatic are the application of psychoanalytic techniques to the biographies of great religious figures seen for example in Erik Erikson's studies of Martin Luther (1958) and Mahatma Gandhi (1969), or William Meissner's study of the founder of the Jesuits, Ignatius Loyola (1992).[36] And placed within a still wider perspective, Freud has proved the creative catalyst in a whole range of critical, and often opposing, re-evaluations of society and religion. In the 1920s and 1930s the discovery of Freud was a decisive feature of Critical Theory in the so-called Frankfurt School of Theodor Adorno (1903-1969) and Max Horkheimer (1895-1973), and this influence has continued in the absorption of Freud into more recent French philosophy, which admittedly the Anglo-Saxon mind has often found hard to take. Here the psychoanalyst Jacques Lacan (1901-1981) is the key figure in the 'structuralist' appropriation of Freud, while his philosophical opponent, Paul Ricoeur (1913-2005) is the principal exponent of Freudian techniques in 'hermeneutical philosophy'. Indeed Ricoeur's monumental *Freud and Philosophy* (1965) is a seminal work in modern assessments of Freud, and it was he, we recall, who placed Freud among the 'masters of suspicion' – the others being Marx and Nieztsche – citing the phenomenon of repression as one of those mechanisms by which the true meaning of cultural symbolism is concealed from view.[37] And once uncovered we find a superfluity of meanings, not to be deciphered solely in the formulae of the sexual impulse. So the Oedipus complex can itself be de-literalized and refashioned in the authoritarian languages of our culture, with the original parental trauma now absorbed and internalized within the moral codes of society, against which the emerging individual must constantly struggle. This allows for a re-assessment of the religious symbols of hope and future transformation not as delusional but as part of a psychical programme of human aspiration and development.

But Freud would give such philosophizing very short shrift. This was not just because he viewed any such dilution of the oedipal trauma as an act of treachery against the greatest achievement of psychoanalysis: it was also because, by resurrecting the dysfunctional illusions of

35 As an extreme example of this process, see Michael P. Carroll, *Catholic Cults and Devotions: A Psychological Inquiry,* Kingston, Montreal, McGill-Queen's University Press, 1989. His first chapter is headed 'The Anal-Erotic Origins of the Rosary'.

36 See Erickson, *Young Man Luther,* New York, Norton, 1958, and *Gandhi's Truth,* New York, Norton, 1969; and W.W. Meissner, *Ignatius of Loyola,* New Haven, Yale University Press, 1992.

37 See above, p.88

religion, however these may be expressed, it treads a regressive path in human self-understanding, establishing an entirely false sense of human empowerment in relation to both the internal and external forces of nature. We should underscore the fact that Freud placed psychoanalysis within a cultural sequence that had gradually dethroned human beings from their pre-eminence within the animal kingdom. Man, to express the matter theologically, could no longer consider himself the special creation of God, made in the divine image (*imago dei*), not least because he had been made to realize that he is hardly master of himself but subject to the hidden impulses of the unconscious mind, of which he is scarcely aware. This was certainly Freud's own estimate of his achievement. Besides psychoanalysis he mentions two other 'death blows' to this narcissistic assertion of human self-esteem: the cosmological blow administered by Copernicus in ending a geocentric view of the world, and the biological blow delivered by Darwin in establishing the animal descent of man. This chapter has added another member to this illustrious group – Karl Marx – who described a similar decentering process by clarifying the extent to which human beings are at the mercy of their material and economic circumstances. The cultural impact of this dethronement cannot be overestimated, and Freud stands as the first and most famous chronicler of its psychological effects. And these effects, as we have seen, circumscribe a tension at the heart of cultural life. For, on the one hand, we find a realistic acceptance of how matters stand – that life is circumscribed by birth and death and that there is nothing else besides – and, on the other, a delusional denial of this unpalatable but nevertheless empirical truth. For Freud, the former is atheistic and rational and asserts the duties of autonomous struggle within these defined limits; and the later is theistic and irrational and infantile because replacing any constructive engagement with reality with the fantasies of another world. This at any rate is how Freud sees it. For him religion offers no opportunities for personal development because the consolations it offers are forever fighting against the reality of the human situation. And the result is the neurosis of wishful-thinking, a mental disorder exhibited in every religious activity.

Conclusion

The three main authors discussed in this chapter – Feurbach, Marx and Freud – subscribe to the wishful-thinking school of atheism. They maintain that the fundamental purpose of religion is to make human life more bearable by making the suffering endured more understandable; and that the believer achieves this by projection: by transforming the natural human desires for protection and self-affirmation into the consolations provided by a benevolent deity. Each of them – and here we should also include Nietzsche – believed therefore that the religious consciousness was self-deceiving because the impulse to faith was in fact generated by powerful forces of which believers themselves were unaware. To this end each of these authors constructs a conceptually elaborate theory that deciphers the religious code by unearthing the link between the outward apparatus of religion – theology and ritual – and these compulsive and unconscious impulses. Thus are the gods unmasked as anthropomorphic objectifications of some internal or subjective human characteristic now given elevated reality, sufficiently magnified as superhuman powers to become the focus of worship. These authors were not of course the first to conceive of the idea of projection. We remember that they belong to a venerable tradition, passing through Hume and d'Holbach, and reaching as far back as the latter half of the sixth century B.C. The Greek poet Xenophanes of Colophon (c.570-c.478) clearly realized that men create their gods as images of themselves, cynically observing that 'the Negroes believe that their gods are flat-nosed and black, the Thracians that theirs have blue eyes and red hair.'[1] To be sure, Feurbach, Marx and Freud conceive of projection in their own way, but in each case the concept is crucial as an explanatory tool: it explains why the gods had come into existence in the first place, why they remain compelling and seductive fantasies of the imagination, and why their disappearance is a necessary step towards individual and social empowerment. They do not, it is true, write off the whole history of religion as a chronicle of wasted time; but it is a narrative nevertheless of the nursery, which the individual advancing to maturity must outgrow.

---

1   Quoted by A.B. Drachmann, *Atheism in Pagan Antiquity*, London, Gyldendal, 1922, p.18.

There are, of course, many other and much more recent theories about the origins of religion, which I cannot mention in any detail here.[2] But it is worth in conclusion pointing to a common feature that is, I think, shared by all. If the acceptance of the religious fantasy is a sign of immaturity, then the corollary is an unreserved acceptance of those responsibilities that come with maturity. The mature individual rejects all theological absolutes and accepts the naturalistic presumption that nothing exists outside a self-sufficient natural order of being. But the theistic hypothesis is not rejected solely on theoretical or methodological grounds: it is rejected on moral grounds as well. Religion, as all our authors make clear, misdirects human resources away from the primary duty of improving the human lot. Focusing on another world inevitably dilutes concern for this world and any attempt to improve it. Human progress thus demands that wishful-thinking gives way to reality-thinking, and requires the substitution of the metaphysical mode of thought with a practical humanism dedicated to the alleviation of human misery and alienation. In this programme of transformation any residual belief in God must be eliminated as a necessary first step; but thereafter it must proceed on the basis that, with nature being all that is, the salvation of the world is circumscribed by the world itself, and that human beings, in the exercise of their individual freedom and creativity, are the principal agents of renewal. For this reason atheism never qualifies its belief, inherited from its Greek ancestors, that the individual is the exclusive measure of meaning and value, who fashions his or her own destiny through the progressive transformation of themselves and their environment. But whether this transformation should be viewed with optimism or pessimism is another matter. Here, as we have seen, atheists divide. But on the whole atheism does not claim for itself a complete panacea for the human condition. The world still reveals its dimensions of cruelty and innocent suffering; and the fact that atheism promotes the autonomous individual as the agent of reform does not mean that his freedom will always be exercised for the greater good and that a state of brotherly love and social justice will

---

2   There are, for example, several modern studies that offer naturalistic accounts of religion in terms of neuroscience, anthropology and evolution. See S. Guthrie, *Faces in the Clouds: A New Theory of Religion*, Oxford, Oxford University Press, 1993; M. Alper, *The "God" Part of the Brain: A Scientific Interpretation of Human Spirituality and God*, Brooklyn, N.Y., Rogue Press, 2001; Pascal Boyer, *Religion Explained: The Evolutionary Origins of Religious Thought*, New York, Basic Books, 2001; D.S. Wilson, *Darwin's Cathedral: Evolution, Religion, and the Nature of Society*, Chicago, University of Chicago Press, 2002; and D.M. Broom, *The Evolution of Morality and Religion*, Cambridge, Cambridge University Press, 2003.

inevitably prevail. Atheism does not substitute one religion for another, and does not replace the belief in God with the belief in man, godless but now deified.

There is one last thing to say. It is a common assumption of religious faith that, without God, life is essentially meaningless and purposeless, with human beings condemned to the depressing and uninviting prospect of the compost heap. And, on the face of it, believers have a point. With the astronomers we must now accept that our earth, far from being a special creation, was formed by accretion from the solar nebula and has a short projected time-life, orbiting a dying sun and set within an ageing solar system; and with the biologists we must also accept that we are not special creatures made in God's image but are part of an evolutionary process, indifferent or even hostile to our needs, with the ape as our ancestor. This is bad enough but worse is to come. For any consolations that we may, quite understandably, look for beyond this gloomy landscape are also denied us. There is no life after death, and so no final meeting with loved ones, no final separation between the just and the unjust, and no system of rewards and punishment to justify us in our belief that good lives are lived by obeying God's commands. There is, then, nothing, absolutely nothing to look forward to. What a contrast this makes to the religious alternative, to the divine scheme of things, in which God endows our lives with purpose from the moment of our birth and inspires in us feelings of love, trust, security and hope. The atheistic alternative cannot compete with this. Nothing comes from nothing, and so how can our lives have any meaning when faced with the inevitability of extinction? Extreme pessimism seems, then, to be the only appropriate attitude to adopt for those who believe that this vale of misery is all we have, that it contains few enjoyments, and that what pleasures there are will be rare, spasmodic and short.

But this is quite wrong and is a slander against the atheistic outlook. It is true that the death of God, as heralded by Nietzsche, marks the end of any belief in any absolute centre of meaning and being, in an unshakable and divine foundation upon which to build our hopes for a heavenly future; but, as Nietzsche continues, pessimism is not, or should not be, the accompanying attitude of mind. To reject the idea that human beings are divine artefacts certainly robs them of an assigned purpose, allocated beyond themselves; but it does not, for all that, detract from life's meaningfulness. It is simply that, with God's death, this meaning has been relocated. To follow Nietzsche again, the antidote to pessimism is an active nihilism or courageous realism, which allows for our joyous acceptance of what this all-too-brief life offers. There may, then, be no overarching purpose to life, but that leaves untouched the purposes of life, those meanings that human beings find for themselves in their interactions with each other and their world. It is not, after all, purposeless to sustain loving relationships, to seek beauty, to educate or care for others, to struggle for peace or to husband our natural resources. All these are purposes created by us precisely in order to maintain a meaningful existence; and whether we are happy or not will largely depend on the extent to which these aims have been achieved. These, then, are the offerings of living that make our lives worthwhile.

Camus, in his famous parable of Sisyphus, expresses this point very well. As a punishment for his disobedience the gods condemn Sisyphus to a life of eternal and hopeless labour: of ceaselessly rolling a rock up a slope, only to see it always crash to the bottom. Nothing could be more terrible than this. Nor is this a condition unknown to us: 'The workman of today works everyday in his life at the same tasks, and his fate is no less absurd.' But Sisyphus is heroic in the acceptance of his lot. For while on one level he is conscious that his life is an absurdity, he is aware on another that it has meaning and value, bringing him joy rather than despair. This happiness derives from Sisyphus' struggle with his rock, with his active determination to overcome his punishment; but it also stems from knowing his rock so well, from his intimacy with it, and from his growing perception of all the delights it contains.

> At that subtle moment when man glances backward over his life, Sisyphus returning toward his rock, in that slight pivoting he contemplates that series of unrelated actions which become his fate, created by him, combined under his memory's eye and soon sealed by his death. Thus, convinced of the wholly human origin of all that is human, a blind man eager to see who knows that the night has no end, he is still on the go. The rock is still rolling.
>
> I leave Sisyphus at the foot of the mountain! One always finds one's burden again. But Sisyphus teaches the higher fidelity that negates the gods and raises rocks. He too concludes that all is well. This universe henceforth without a master seems to him neither sterile nor futile. Each atom of that stone, each mineral flake of that night filled mountain, in itself forms a world. The struggle itself toward the heights is enough to fill a man's heart. One must imagine Sisyphus happy.[3]

---

3   *TAC*: 242

Guide to Further Reading

Chapter 1

Beattie, Tina. *The New Atheists*, London, Darton, Longman & Todd, 2007.

Berman, David. *A History of Atheism in Britain from Hobbes to Russell*, London & New York, Routledge 1988.

Baggini, Julian. *Atheism: A Very Short Introduction*, Oxford, Oxford University Press, 2003.

Buckley, Michael J. *At the Origins of Modern Atheism*. New Haven, Yale University Press, 1987.

Everitt, Nicholas. *The Non-Existence of God*, London & New York, Routledge, 2004.

Flint, Robert. *Agnosticism*, Edinburgh, William Blackwood, 1903

Gaskin, J.C.A. (ed.) *Varieties of Unbelief*, London, Collier Macmillan, 1989.

Joshi, S.T. *The Agnostic Reader*, Buffalo, New York, Prometheus Books, 2007.

Le Poidevin, Robin. *Arguing for Atheism*, Routledge, London & New York, 1996.

Martin, Michael. *Atheism*, Philadelphia, Temple University Press, 1990.

————. (ed.). *The Cambridge Companion to Atheism*, Cambridge, Cambridge University Press, 2007.

MacIntyre, Alasdair (with Paul Ricoeur). *The Religious Significance of Atheism*, New York, 1969.

Robertson. *History of Freethought in the Nineteenth Century*, London, Dawsons, 1969

Royle, Edward. *Victorian Infidels: The Origins of the British Secularist Movement,1791-1866*, Manchester, University of Manchester Press, 1974.

Smith, George H. *Atheism: The Case against God*, Buffalo, New York, Prometheus Books, 1989.

Stein, Gordon. *The Encyclopedia of Unbelief*, Buffalo, New York, Prometheus Books, 1985.

Thrower, James. *Western Atheism: A Short History*, Buffalo, New York, Prometheus Books, 2000.

Chapter 2

Annas, Julia (with Jonathan Barnes). *The Modes of Scepticism*, Cambridge University Press, Cambridge, 1985.

Bailey Cyril. *The Greek Atomists and Epicurus*, Clarendon Press, Oxford, 1928

————. *The Religion of Ancient Rome*, London, Constable, 1907.

Barnes, J. *The Presocratic Philosophers*, London, Routledge, 1982.

Beard, M. (ed., with J. North, and S. Price). *Religions of Rome*, vols. 1 and 2, Cambridge 1998).

Burnet, J. *Early Greek Philosophy*, Kessinger Publishing, 2003.

Burnyeat, Myles (ed.). *The Skeptical Tradition*, Berkeley, University of California Press, 1983.

Burkert, W. *Greek Religion*, trans. W. Raffan, Oxford, 1985.

Cartledge, Paul. *Democritus*, London, Routledge, 1999.

Easterling, P.E (ed., with J.V. Muir). *Greek Religion and Society*, Cambridge, Cambridge University Press,, 1985

Festugière, A.J. *Personal Religion among the Greeks*, Berkeley, University of California Press, 1954.

Gaskin, John (ed.). *The Epicurean Philosophers*, London, Everyman, 1905.

Guthrie W.K. *The Greeks and their Gods*, London, Methuen, 1950

————. *The Religion and Mythology of the Greeks*, Cambridge, Cambridge University Press, 1964.

Hicks, R.D. *Stoic and Epicurean*, New York, Russell and Russell, 1962.

Keys, Madeleine. *Sextus Empiricus and Ancient Scepticism*, Austin, Texas, University Of Texas at Austin, 1990.

Long, A.A. *Hellenistic Philosophy: Stoics, Epicureans, Sceptics*, Berkeley, University of California Press, 1986.

Naess, Arne. *Scepticism*, New York, Humanities Press, 1969.

Nilsson, M.P. *Greek Folk Religion*, Columbia, 1940

Popkin, Richard. *The History of Skepticism from Erasmus to Descartes*, New York, Harper Torchbacks. 1964.

Sharples, R.W. *Stoics, Epicureans and Sceptics*, London, Routledge, 1996.

Scheid, J. *An Introduction to Roman Religion*, trans. Janet Lloyd, Edinburgh, Edinburgh University Press, 2003

Stewart, Z. *Essays on Religion and the Ancient World*, Oxford, Clarendon Press, 1972.

Stough, Charlotte. *Greek Skepticism*, Berkeley, 1969.

Chapter 3

Atkins, P.W. *Creation Revisited*, Oxford, W.H. Freeman, 1992.

Barrow, J. (with F. Tipler). *The Anthropic Cosmological Principle*, Oxford, Oxford University Press, 1988.

Davis, Stephen T. *God, Reason and Theistic Proofs*, Edinburgh, Edinburgh University Press, 1997.

Dawkins, Richard. *A Devil's Chaplain: Selected Essays*, London, Weidenfeld & Nicolson, 2003.

————. *Climbing Mount Improbable*, New York, Norton, 1996.

————. *River out of Eden*, London, Weidenfeld & Nicolson, 1995.

————. *The Blind Watchmaker*, Harlow, Longman, 1986.

————. *The God Delusion*, London, Bantam Press, 2006.

————. *The Selfish Gene*, Oxford, Oxford University Press, 1976.

————. 'Universal Darwinism', *Evolution from Molecules to Men*, ed D.S. Bendall, Cambridge, Cambridge University Press. 1983, pp. 403-25.

————. *Unweaving the Rainbow*, London, Penguin, 1998.

Dennett, Daniel C. *Darwin's Dangerous Idea*, London, Allen Lane, The Penguin Press, 1995.

————. *Breaking the Spell: Religion as a Natural Phenomenoni*, London, Viking, 2006.

Mackie, J.L. *The Miracle of Theism*, Oxford, Clarendon Press, 1982.

Manson, Neil (ed.). *God and Design: The Teleological Argument and Modern Science*, London, Routledge, 2003.

Matson, Wallace. *The Existence of God*, Ithaca, Cornell University Press, 1965.

Ross, Hugh. *Beyond the Cosmos: What Recent Discoveries in Astronomy and Physics Reveal about the Nature of God*, Colorado Springs, Nav Press, 1996.

Stenger, V.J. *Has Science found God?* New York, Prometheus Books, 2003.

————. *Not by Design: The Origins of the Universe*, Amherst, N.Y., Prometheus Books, 1988.

Wolpert, Lewis *Six Impossible Things before Breakfast*, London, Faber, 2006.

Chapter 4

Adams, Marilyn & Robert (eds.). *The Problem of Evil*, Oxford, Oxford University Press, 1979.

Davies, Brian. *The Reality of God and the Problem of Evil*, London & New York, Continuum, 2006.

Davis, Stephen (ed.). *Encountering Evil*, Atlanta, Knox Press, 1981.

Farrer, Austin. *Love Almighty and Ills Unlimited*, London, Collins, 1962.

Geach, P.T. *Providence and Evil*, Cambridge, Cambridge University Press, 1977.

Geivett, Douglas. *Evil and the Evidence for God: The Challenge of John Hick's Theodicy*, Philadelphia, Temple University Press, 1995.

Howard-Snyder, Daniel (ed.). *The Evidential Argument from Evil*, Bloomington and Indianapolis, Indiana University Press, 1996.

Lewis, C.S. *The Problem of Pain*, New York, Macmillan, 1962.

Mathis, Terry. *Against John Hick: An Examination of his Philosophy of Religion*, New York, University Press of America, 1985.

McCloskey, H.J. *God and Evil*, The Hague, Martinus Nijhoff, 1974.

Palmer, Michael. *The Philosophy of Religion*, Vol. 1, Cambridge, The Lutterworth Press, 2008, pp.130-213.

Peterson, Michael (ed.). *The Problem of Evil*, Notre Dame, Indiana, University of Notre Dame Press, 1992.

Pike, Nelson. *God and Evil: Readings on the Theological Problem of Evil*, Englewood Cliffs, Prentice-Hall, 1964.

Raeder, Linda. *John Stuart Mill and the Religion of Humanity*, Columbia & London, University of Missouri Press, 2002.

Reichenbach, Bruce. *Evil and a Good God*, New York, Fordham University Press, 1982.

Rowe, William. *Can God be Free?* Oxford, Oxford University Press, 2004.

Sutherland, Stewart. *Atheism and the Rejection of God: Contemporary Philosophy and the Brothers Karamazov*, Oxford, Blackwell, 1977.

Swinburne, Richard. *Providence and the Problem of Evil*, Oxford, Clarendon Press, 1998.

Chapter 5

Altizer, Thomas. *The New Gospel of Christian Atheism*, Aurora, Colo.: Davies Publishing, 2002.

————. (with William Hamilton). *Radical Theology and the Death of God*, Indianapolis, Bibbs-Merrill Press, 1966.

Barrett, William. *What is Existentialism*, New York, Grove Press, 1964.

Cooper, David E. *Existentialism*, Oxford, Basil Blackwell, 1990.

Diener, Paul W. *Religion and Morality*, Louisville, John Knox Press, 1997.

Golomb, Jacob. *In Search of Authenticity*, London & New York, Routledge, 1995.

Grayling, A.C. *What is Good?* London, Weidenfeld & Nicolson, 2003.

Hollingdale, R.J. *Nietzsche: The Man and His Philosophy*, London, Ark Paperbacks, 1985.

Holloway, Richard. *Godless Morality: Keeping Religion out of Ethics*, Edinburgh, Canongate Books, 1999.

Kaufmann, Walter. *Existentialism, Religion, and Death*, New York, New American Library, 1976.

————. *The Basic Writings of Nietzsche*, New York, Random House, 1968.

————. *The Portable Nietzsche*, New York, Viking Press, 1968.

————. *Nietzsche: Philosopher, Psychologist, Antichrist*, Princeton, Princeton University Press, 1974.

Leiter, Brian. *Nietzsche on Morality*, London, Routledge, 2002

Lewy, Guenter. *If God is Dead, Everything is Permitted?* Edison, NJ. Transaction Publishers, 2008.

Onfray, Michel. *In Defence of Atheism*, translated by Jeremy Leggatt. London, Profile Books, 2007.

Robinson, Richard. *An Atheist's Values*, Oxford, Basil Blackwell, 1964.

Russell, Bertrand. *Russell on Religion*, ed., Louis Greenspan & Stefan Andersson, London & New York, 1999 ***

————. *Bertrand Russell on God and Religion*, ed. Al Seckel, New York, Buffalo, Prometheus Books, 2000.

Wainright, William J. *Religion and Morality*, Aldershot, Ashgate, 2005.

Young, Julian. *Nietzsche's Philosophy of Religion*, Cambridge, Cambridge University Press, 2006.

Chapter 6

Basinger, David and Randall. *Philosophy and Miracle*, Lewiston, The Edwin Mellen Press, 1986.

Brown, Colin. *Miracles and the Critical Mind*, Grand Rapids, Mich., Eerdmana, 1983.

Burns, R.M. *The Great Debate on Miracles: From Granville to David Hume*, Lewisburg. Bucknell University Press, 1981.

Earman, John. *Hume's Abject Failure: The Argument from Miracles*, Oxford, Oxford University Press, 2000.

Flew, Antony. *Hume's Philosophy of Belief*, London, Routledge & Kegan Paul, 1961.

Fruchtmann, Jack. *Thomas Paine and the Religion of Nature*, John Hopkins University Press, 1993

Harvey, Van. *The Historian and the Believer*, London, SCM Press, 1967.

Houston, J. *Reported Miracles: A Critique of Hume*, Cambridge, Cambridge University Press, 1994

Lewis, C.S. *Miracles*, London, Collins, 1947, edition 1960

Nickell, Joe. *Looking for a Miracle*. Amherst, New York, Prometheus Books, 1993.

Palmer, Michael. *The Philosophy of Religion: A Commentary and Sourcebook*, Volume 1, Cambridge, Lutterworth Press, 2008, pp. 215-283.

————. *The Question of God*, London, Routledge, 2001, pp.171-226.

Strauss, Leo. *Spinoza's Critique of Religion*, Chicago, University of Chicago Press, 1997.

Swinburne, Richard (ed). *Miracles*, London, Collier Macmillan, 1989.

Tennant, F.R. *Miracles and its Philosophical Presuppositions*, Cambridge, Cambridge University Press, 1925.

Tweyman, Stanley (ed.). *Hume on Miracles*, Bristol, Thoemmes Press, 1996.

Williams, T.C. *The Idea of the Miraculous*, London, Macmillan, 1990.

Yandell, Keith. *Hume's 'Inexplicable Mystery': His Views on Religion*, Philadelphia, Temple University Press, 1990.

Chapter 7

Bainton, Michael (ed.). *Anthropological Approaches to the Study of Religion*, London, Tavistock, 1966.

Capps, Donald. *Freud and Freudians on Religion*, New Haven & London, Yale University Press, 2001.

Fromm, Erich. *Beyond the Chains of Illusion: My Encounter with Marx and Freud*, London, Sphere Books, 1962.

Harvey, Van (ed.). *Feuerbach and the Interpretation of Religion*, Cambridge, Cambridge University Press, 1997.

Kamenka, Eugene. *The Philosophy of Ludwig Feuerbach*, New York, Praeger, 1970.

Kung, Hans. *Freud and the Problem of God*, New Haven, Yale University Press, 1990.

Marx, Karl. *Marx on Religion*, ed. John Raines, Philadelphia, Temple University Press, 2002.

McLellan, David. *Marxism and Religion*, London, Macmillan, 1987.

McKown, D.B. *The Classical Marxist Critiques of Religion: Marx, Engels, Lenin, Kautsky*, The Hague, Martinus Nijhoff, 1975.

Morris, Brian. *Anthropological Studies of Religion*, Cambridge, Cambridge University Press, 1993.

Palmer, Michael. *Freud and Jung on Religion*, London, Routledge, 1997.

Preuss, J. Samuel. *Explaining Religion: Criticism and Theory from Bodin to Freud*, New Haven, Yale University Press, 1987.

Raines, John. *Marx on Religion*, Philadelphia, Pa.: Temple University Press, 2002.

Suckiel, Ellen Kappy. *Heaven's Champion: William James's Philosophy of Religion*, Notre Dame, Ind., University of Notre Dame Press, 1996.

Wartofsky, Marx W. *Feuerbach*, Cambridge. Cambridge University Press, 1977.

Wheen, Francis, *Karl Marx: A Life*, London, Fourth Estate, 1999.

Index of Names

Index of Subjects